アートと都市を巡る
横浜⇔台北
藝術與都市 橫濱與台北
Art and City in Yokohama and Taipei

アートと都市を巡る横浜と台北

日本と台湾は古くから、様々なもの（都市、環境、文化、教育など）を共有しながら歩んできました。正式な国交がない現在でも、都市レベル、民間レベルの交流は盛んです。そんな状況のなか、2005年、横浜市と台北市が推進し、様々な部門で都市間の新たな交流プロジェクトを開始しました。そのひとつが「BankART1929」と「台北国際芸術村（TAV）」の芸術部門の交流です。お互いの都市（施設）に作家が3ヶ月間滞在しながら制作を行なうという、交換アーティストインレジデンス（AIR）。このプログラムをこれまで10年間続けてきました。AIRは、人と人（都市と都市）との信頼関係を時間をかけて培っていく魅力あるプログラムですが、成果物の発表ということに関してはあまり力点をおいていませんので、外の世界に対しては少しわかり難い部分もあります。

そこで、10年目をむかえたこともあり、関係する日台の作家21名による、大規模な展覧会を企画してみました。アーティストは、異国に滞在することで、何を考えているのか、何を行っているのか、自身はどう変わったのか、あるいは周辺とどういった化学反応をおこしたのか。アーティストたちの「生活すること」と「発表すること」の両断面をこの展覧会から感じとっていただければと思います。

同時代の都市とアートを巡り、新しい日台の関係が構築できることを願います。

Art and City in Yokohama and Taipei

Whether in urban development, environmental matters, culture or education links between Japan and Taiwan are deeply entrenched. While no formal diplomatic relations between both nations are in place, their long-abiding relationship nonetheless thrives on an inter-city and private level. Given this high level of co-operation, Yokohama and Taipei initiated a series of exchanges projects in 2005. Amongst these was the artist exchange programme between BankART and the Taipei Artist Village, in which the host city or institution offers a residency to a visiting artist for three months during which period they create a work in-situ under the auspices of the Artist in Residence (AIR) programme. This programme now celebrates its tenth year in operation.

Over time the AIR programme has bolstered the relationship between the citizens and the institutions in both cities. However, given that to date it hasn't put too much emphasis on concrete results, the programme remains a little incomprehensible to those from outside. To overcome this, we decided to try and organise the 10th anniversary of this programme with a large-scale exhibition featuring twenty-one Japanese and Taiwanese artists. As the participating artists confront life in a residency abroad, they deal with a myriad of issues on a daily basis; their changing thoughts, their sense of direction in a foreign city, the transformations they undergo or how they chemically respond to new surroundings. This exhibition will take a dual pronged approach, allowing the visitor to at once glimpse how the artists live and express themselves.

We hope this exhibition concentrating on urban culture and art will form the basis for new avenues of co-operation between Japan and Taiwan.

藝術與都市 橫濱與台北

日本與台灣，在都市、環境、文化、教育等諸多領域有著長期的交流與合作。現在，雖未正式建交，但都市之間、民間層面的交流十分活躍。2005年起，橫濱與台北在各領域開展了都市間的交流新項目。「BankART1929」與「台北國際藝術村」的藝術交流就是其中之一。兩市藝術家互換，分別進行為期3個月的駐村創作，這就是Artist In Residence(AIR)。該項目已連續舉辦了10年。AIR極具魅力，十分注重長時間建立起來的人與人（都市與都市）之間的信賴關係，然而至今在成果發表、信息發布方面較為薄弱。

因此，在迎來10周年之際，我們策劃了由21名日台相關藝術家參加的大型展覽。藝術家們在異國他鄉，思考了什麼？做了些什麼？自身發生了怎樣的變化？與周邊互相又產生了怎樣的影響？希望通過本次展覽，大家能對藝術家們的「日常生活」與「作品發表」兩個層面有所了解。

我們衷心希望，通過同一時代的「藝術與都市」這一主題，建立日台新關係。

「都市とアートを巡る横浜と台北」
会場：BankART Studio NYK（全館）
日程：2015年7月24日［金］〜9月13日［日］
休館日：8月13日［木］〜18日［火］
時間：11:00〜19:00（最終日は17:00まで）
主催：BankART1929
共催：横浜市文化観光局
協力：台北国際芸術村（TAV）、台北市
助成：芸術文化振興基金

Art and City in Yokohama and Taipei Exhibition

Venue : BankART Studio NYK
Dates : 24 July 2015 –13 September 2015
Exceptionally closed between 13 August thru August 18.
Time : 11:00 to 19:00 (Final day closes at 17:00)
Presented by BankART1929
Co-organized by Yokohama City Culture and Tourism Bureau
Cooperation : Taipei Artist Village (TAV), Taipei City
Assistance from the Japan Arts Council

"藝術與都市 橫濱與台北"
地點：BankART Studio NYK（全館）
時間：2015年7月24日（周五）〜9月13日（周日）
　　　11:00〜19:00（9月13日17:00結束）
閉館日：2015年8月13日（周四）〜18日（周二）
主辦：BankART1929
共同主辦：橫濱市文化觀光局
協辦：台北國際藝術村（TAV）、台北市
資助：藝術文化振興基金

CONTENT

010 **BankART 1929**

012 **Taipei Artist Village = TAV**

014 台北市・横浜市アーティスト交流プログラム
The Artist Exchange Program Between Taipei and Yokohama

2005-2014

2005
Yokohama → Taipei
016 オフニブロール Off Nibroll
Taipei → Yokohama
022 陳 妍伊 Chen Yen-Yi

2006
Yokohama → Taipei
028 東野哲史 Higashino Tetsushi
Taipei → Yokohama
034 賴 珮瑜 Lai Pei-Yu

2007
Yokohama → Taipei
040 村田峰紀 Murata Mineki
Taipei → Yokohama
046 何 明桂 Ho Ming-Kuei

2008
Yokohama → Taipei
052 川瀬浩介 Kawase Kohske
Taipei → Yokohama
058 陳 宛伶 Chen Wan-ling

2009
Yokohama → Taipei
064 井出賢嗣 Ide Kenji
Taipei → Yokohama
070 周 育正 Chou Yu-Cheng

2010
Yokohama → Taipei
076 伊佐治雄悟 Isaji Yugo
Taipei → Yokohama
082 陳 怡慧 Chen Yi-Huei

2011
Yokohama → Taipei
088 幸田千依 Koda Chie
Taipei → Yokohama
094 羅 仕東 Lo Shih-Tung

2012
Yokohama → Taipei
100 松田直樹 Matsuda Naoki
Taipei → Yokohama
106 羅 懿君 Lo Yi-Chun

2013
Yokohama → Taipei
112 磯崎道佳 Isozaki Michiyoshi
Taipei → Yokohama
118 楊 子弘 Yang Tzu-Hung

2014
Yokohama → Taipei
124 サンドラム SUNDRUM
Taipei → Yokohama
130 許 喬彥 Hsu Chiao-Yen

2008 Special Recognition
Yokohama → Taipei
136 丸山純子 Maruyama Junko

BankART Studio NYK

BankART1929

歴史的建造物等を文化芸術に活用し、都心部再生の起点にしていこうとする横浜市の創造都市構想のひとつ。2004年3月に元銀行の建物二棟を核に実験事業としてスタート。スタジオ、スクール、カフェパブ、ショップ、コンテンツ制作をベースにしながら、アート、建築、パフォーマンス等、多岐にわたる主催・コーディネート事業を展開してきた。2006年度からは「経済的基盤の確立」「他都市及び国際的なネットワークの構築」「創造界隈のパイオニア的存在としての自覚」という指標のもと、本格事業へと移行。

現在は、日本郵船の湾岸倉庫を活用したBankART Studio NYKを中心にBankART妻有等の3つのサテライトを拠点に活動を行っている。「地震EXPO」等の他分野との協働や、北仲B&Wや本町ビル45等、周辺の空きビルへのクリエイター誘致、「Landmark Project」「食と現代美術」「大野一雄フェス」等の街への展開を通して、創造界隈形成の一翼を担っている。

The City of Yokohama started the BankART1929 as one of the projects of regenerating the energy of the metropolitan area by reusing the historical buildings for the cultural and artistic purposes. It began in March of 2004 for a two years experimental project in the former bank buildings. The BankART1929 remains active in organizing and supporting many different projects yearly, crossing genres of the arts, architecture, performance, music etc., as well as running the artist residency, school, café-pub and bookshop, and the contents production. In 2006, the project was decided to be continued as one of the major cultural projects and encouraged to achieve the financial independence, to build the network among the cities and the nations and to play the leading role in the creative neighborhood. The current project includes the BankART Studio NYK using Nippon Yusen Warehouse, the BankART Tsumari and additional 3 satellite sites. The recent entrepreneurial activities are : the Earthquake EXPO and other exhibitions fusing the different genres, the Kitanaka B&W and Honcho Shigokai utilizing the empty buildings for creators ateliers, as well as the Landmark Project, Food and Contemporary Arts and Kazuo Ohno Festival that mainly happen in the streets and outdoor spaces, thus contribute to promoting the creative neighborhood.

Taipei Artist Village

Taipei Artist Village = TAV

台北国際芸術村(TAV)は市の中心地に位置し、都市の様々なネットワークに緊密にリンクし、交通もたいへん便利な場所。ここは、アーティストが創造性をより大きな世界に広げる場として充分な機能を備えている。なにより都市の真ん中にあることで、地域の参加を促し活力を得ることができ、台北市と世界との創造的な交流の架け橋になっている。2001年台北市文化局は、芸術が社会に対して持つ役割を全うする施設をつくる目的でこのTAVを設立した。また、2010年には宝蔵巌国際芸術村(THAV)をオープンさせた。これらはアーティストの滞在制作と放棄された建物の再生という施策によって運営されている。世界中からアーティストが参加し、地域のアーティストやコミュニティと交流を深めることで、アーティストが生活し、制作する場所であるだけでなく、交流の場となり、文化の発展と革新に大きく寄与している。国際芸術村のミッションは、Arts-in-Residence Taipei (AIR Taipei)プログラムを実行し、展覧会や公演を主催することである。2014年末迄に、58ヶ国から391人のアーティストが、台北国際芸術村(TAV)と宝蔵巌国際芸術村(THAV)に滞在制作し、145人の台湾人アーティストが交換プログラムにより世界各地でレジデンスに参加している。

Situated in the city center with convenient transportation and a comprehensive network of urban facilities, Taipei Artist Village is the consummate base for artists to expand the hinterland of their creativity toward the wider world. Its imminent accessibility enables the participation and vitality of the local community, forming a bridge of creative exchange between Taipei City and the globe. The Taipei City Department of Cultural Affairs founded Taipei Artist Village in 2001 and Treasure Hill Artist Village in 2010 with the intent of fulfilling the responsibilities that the arts have to society, by enacting an artist-in-residence program and revitalizing a derelict space. As international artists took up residence, engaging in exchanges with local arts groups and the community, TAV became not only a place where they could live and make art, but also a bridge of cultural diversity, undertaking the mission of cultural development and innovation.The mission of Taipei Artist Village is to host the Arts-in-Residence Taipei (AIR Taipei) program, and to present art exhibitions and performances. As of the end of 2014, a total of 391 artists from 58 countries have lived and worked at Taipei Artist Village and Treasure Hill Artist Village, and 145 Taiwanese artists have participated in sister programs all over the world as part of AIR Taipei.

台北市・横浜市アーティスト交流プログラム
The Artist Exchange Program Between
Taipei and Yokohama

2005-2014

Taipei Artist Village = TAV

台北国際芸術村(TAV)は市の中心地に位置し、都市の様々なネットワークに緊密にリンクし、交通もたいへん便利な場所。ここは、アーティストが創造性をより大きな世界に広げる場として充分な機能を備えている。なにより都市の真ん中にあることで、地域の参加を促し活力を得ることができ、台北市と世界との創造的な交流の架け橋になっている。2001年台北市文化局は、芸術が社会に対して持つ役割を全うする施設をつくる目的でこのTAVを設立した。また、2010年には宝蔵巌国際芸術村(THAV)をオープンさせた。これらはアーティストの滞在制作と放棄された建物の再生という施策によって運営されている。世界中からアーティストが参加し、地域のアーティストやコミュニティと交流を深めることで、アーティストが生活し、制作する場所であるだけでなく、交流の場となり、文化の発展と革新に大きく寄与している。国際芸術村のミッションは、Arts-in-Residence Taipei (AIR Taipei)プログラムを実行し、展覧会や公演を主催することである。2014年末迄に、58ヶ国から391人のアーティストが、台北国際芸術村(TAV)と宝蔵巌国際芸術村(THAV)に滞在制作し、145人の台湾人アーティストが交換プログラムにより世界各地でレジデンスに参加している。

Situated in the city center with convenient transportation and a comprehensive network of urban facilities, Taipei Artist Village is the consummate base for artists to expand the hinterland of their creativity toward the wider world. Its imminent accessibility enables the participation and vitality of the local community, forming a bridge of creative exchange between Taipei City and the globe. The Taipei City Department of Cultural Affairs founded Taipei Artist Village in 2001 and Treasure Hill Artist Village in 2010 with the intent of fulfilling the responsibilities that the arts have to society, by enacting an artist-in-residence program and revitalizing a derelict space. As international artists took up residence, engaging in exchanges with local arts groups and the community, TAV became not only a place where they could live and make art, but also a bridge of cultural diversity, undertaking the mission of cultural development and innovation.The mission of Taipei Artist Village is to host the Arts-in-Residence Taipei (AIR Taipei) program, and to present art exhibitions and performances. As of the end of 2014, a total of 391 artists from 58 countries have lived and worked at Taipei Artist Village and Treasure Hill Artist Village, and 145 Taiwanese artists have participated in sister programs all over the world as part of AIR Taipei.

台北市・横浜市アーティスト交流プログラム
The Artist Exchange Program Between
Taipei and Yokohama
2005-2014

2005
横浜 ⇒ 台北
Yokohama → Taipei

Off Nibroll
オフニブロール

Nibrollの映像・高橋啓祐と振付家・矢内原美邦によるユニット。劇場をはじめ、美術館やパブリックスペースなど多様な空間で作品を発表。映像インスタレーションとともにダンスパフォーマンスも展開し、身体と映像の関係性を追求している。BankART1929、せんだいメディアテーク、イタリアIerimonti Gallery、GALLERIA FUMAGALLIなどでの個展をはじめ、上海ビエンナーレなど横浜を拠点に国内外で作品を発表している。

Comprising the video artist Keisuke Takahashi and the choreographer Mikuni Yanaihara, Off-Nibroll is active in theatre as well as in museums and public spaces. Incorporating video-installation and dance, their work continually strives to explore the links the relationship between the body and image. Based in Yokohama, they have performed both locally and overseas: BankART1929, Sendai Mediateque, Ierimonti Gallery in Italy, Galleria Fumagalli, and Shanghai Biennale

台北での滞在について

今回の台北国際芸術村での滞在を通して、3ヶ月間余りの短い期間でしたが、多くの人と出会い、多くのことを学び、アーティストとしてこれからどのような立場で創作に挑んでいくかを考えることができました。台湾と日本、そして中国など、アジア各国の関係は一言では片付けられない複雑な問題を孕んでいますが、お互いの国の立場や文化、歴史などの相違から起きてしまう誤解と、それらを越えたところにある共通の観念とを同時に発見することができたと思います。これらはたとえ短い期間であっても、実際に生活者として、そこに住まなければ穫られないことと思いますし、今回の経験はこれからのわたしたちの作品づくりにも、少なからず影響を与えることと思います。これからそれらをどう作品に反映し、観る者に伝えていくかがわたしたちに課せられた義務だと思って、これからも広く制作活動に力を入れていきたいと思っています。

Off Nibroll (2006年3月)

About the stay in TAV

It was only a three months short stay but very rewarding because we met many people and learned a lot about the attitude of how we should face the creation as an artist. It is true that there are some delicate situations among Asian countries, including the relationship of Tawan, Japan and China, but we realized how the misunderstanding is caused by the cultural gaps and different historical backgrounds, and at the same time found the common base beyond the misleading.

Though our stay was so short, we were given the direct and precious experiences by living the life there, and believe that it will have much impact on our ongoing creative activities. After all, it is our obligation to relect how we can materialize the personal experiences into the piece to transfer its hidden meaning to audience, and we will be trying to do it hard.

Off Nibroll (March 2006)

上海・台北・北京メディアアート展
「越界：城市影舞 台北上海雙城記」
The Media Art Exhibition in Shanghai, Taipei, Beijing
Border Crossing : The Shadow Dance Cities

16 December 2005 - 22 January 2006
TAV 1F/百里廳 Barry room

Off Nibroll 滞在成果発表
Off Nibroll: The recital event of the residence program
21 January 2006
TAV 4F/Tea Room

2005
台北 ⇒ 横浜
Taipe → Yokohama

Chen Yen-Yi
陳 妍伊

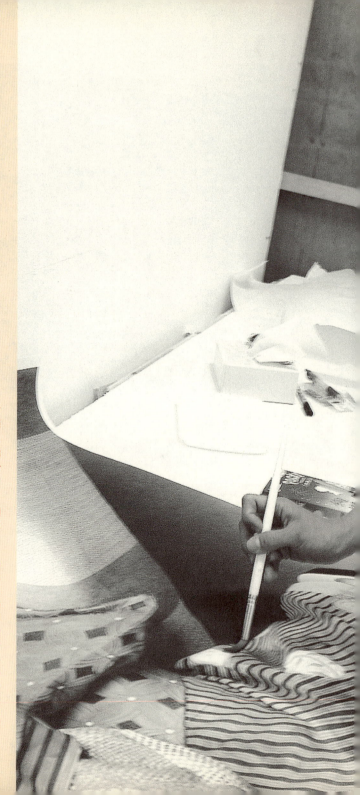

国立台南芸術大学応用芸術大学院修士課程卒業。2000年、第27回台北美術展台北芸術賞にノミネートされる。BankART1929 (2005)、S-AIR (2007)、Anderson Ranch Art Center (米国 2009)、Whitireia (ニュージーランド/2014) で滞在制作を行った。
近年の個展に「Country of Origin」(Whitireia/2014)、「In Transit」(台北/2015) 等。

Graduated from the Tainan National University of the Arts Applied Arts graduate master's program. In 2000, she was nominated for the 27th Taipei Art Exhibition Taipei Arts Award. She has partaken in residency programmes at BankART1929 (2005), S-AIR (2007), Anderson Ranch Art Center (USA, 2009), Whitireia (New Zealand, 2014). Her most recent solo exhibitions include *Country of Origin* (Whitireia / 2014) and *In Transit* (Taipei / 2015).

日本翦影（影の断片コラージュ）
—心の中にある輪廓
Collage of Manipulated Silhouette of Japan
- Hidden Forms in the Heart
24 December 2005 - 7 January 2006
BankART Studio NYK /Studio #5

現代的で賑やかな日本の街を歩くと、時々、着物姿の婦人や若い女の子に出会えます。彼女たちの歩みはとても軽快です。…素焼きの陶製のアップル。それは、壊れやすい生命体を象徴します。日本の生活の中にも同じような不安、心配、焦燥が存在するのだと思います。このような落ち着かなさや不安感から解放されるには、恐らく和服にくるまれて保護され、そして、群衆と一緒になるしかないのだと私には思えました。

私は日本に滞在した3ヶ月間という短い生活体験を、日本食や伝統的な服装をシンプルに組合せることで、日本人の心の深いところにある輪郭と形を浮かび上がらせたいと思います。それは自分の心の中にある日本に対する憧れや印象でもあります。日本人の生活様式と几帳面な態度を象徴することと同時に、日本文化の粘り強さと嗜好を表現したいと思います。

陳妍伊（2005年12月）

Even when you walk around in the modernized and crowded streets in Japan, you can sometimes find ladies as well as younger people in kimono. They seem very enjoyable with the costume.

In the piece, the unglazed ceramic apples symbolize the fragile body of living life. I feel that in the Japanese people's life there may be the similar crisis, anxiety, and impatience as in the fake apples.

And I thought that in order to be free from the discomfort and uneasiness, they need to be dressed and protected with kimono and to get into the mob.

I think that I will materialize my experiences for the 3 months stay in Japan by the simplified installation of the Japanese food along with the traditional costumes, so that I would like to depict the hidden forms people here have in the depth of the heart. I hope that this installation can symbolize the Japanese life style and their well ordered attitude, as well as express the strength and taste of the Japanese culture.

Chen Yen-Yi (December 2005)

2006
横浜 ⇒ 台北
Yokohama → Taipei

Higashino Tetsushi
東野哲史

1976年滋賀県生まれ。武蔵野美術大学造形学部空間演出デザイン学科卒業。非生産的生産活動という名目のもと、日常の取るに足らないものごとや単なる思いつきに対してのレスポンスを制作の起点として、インスタレーション、ビデオ、Web、パフォーマンスなど、メディアを問わず展開する。

Born in Shiga prefecture in 1976, Higashino graduated in scenic design from the faculty of Art and Design at the Musashino Art University. He uses his responses to trivial incidents as a starting point to expand the horizons of his multi-media works, embracing installation, video, web and performance.

台北国際芸術村での滞在について

日常生活をおくる中でのちょっとしたひっかかりに対してのリアクション。これが私の制作の原点であり、私はそれを「非生産的生産活動」と呼んでいます。つまり、取るに足らないものごとの価値の再考です。

台北での3ヶ月という短い滞在期間のなかで、はたしてそのような出来事に遭遇し、即座に制作に反映できるのか？日本語もままならぬというのに言葉が通じない異国の地での生活を当初は危ぶまれたものでした。それほどこの3ヶ月間は私にとって大きな挑戦でした。

しかしそんな不安を払拭するような、とにかく新鮮で好奇心くすぐる、あるいは日本であれ台湾であれ世界中のどこであっても変わらぬであろうと再認識させられるものごと、また多くの友人たちとの出会いは、確実に、私の制作に良い影響を与えてくれました。今改めて、それら全てに感謝しつつ、糧に、更なる前進をするよりほかありません。

東野哲史（2007年3月）

About stay in Taipei Artist Village

The reaction towards what is deemed unimportant in our everyday lives comes into focus.

This interaction plays an essential role in my creative output; I refer to it as a 'non-productive productivity.' In other words, it acts as a stimulus to re-evaluate what are generally considered as life's small things. During my short three month sojourn in Taipei, initially I had some misgivings as to how I would encounter with such 'insignificant' things, and what immediate effect they would have upon my output. Actually I was so anxious about copping with life in a foreign country, given that even my native tongue, Japanese, was still somewhat difficult for me. Therefore, the three months stay abroad was quite a challenge for me.

In any case, the encounters I had with the curious matters in Taipei calmed my disquiet, and I only re-discovered that nothing essentially changed whether one was working in Japan, in Taipei or wherever in the world for that matter. Moreover, the meetings with the many friends there certainly had an enriching effect upon my work. Even now I remain full of gratitude towards all of them; these encounters have been both a vital and indispensable step in my evolution.

Tetsushi Higashino (March 2007)

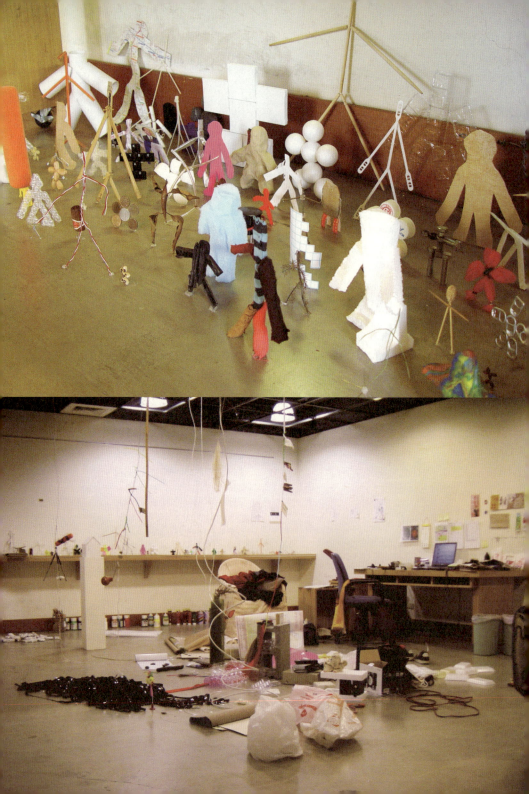

グループ展「圏」
Group Exhibition "Loop"
William Attaway（アメリカ）、黃心健（台湾）、Megan Keating（オーストラリア）、奥村雄樹（日本）、東野哲史（日本）
February 5 — April 8, 2007
TAV 1F／百里廳 Barry room

2006
台北 ⇒ 横浜
Taipe → Yokohama
Lai Pei-Yu
賴 珮瑜

1976年台北に生まれる。国立台南芸術大学造形美術大学院卒業、現在博士課程に在籍。代表作のCity Seriesでは、ドットを駆使しながら、異なる場所での都市景観の相似性が独自の解釈で示され、現在の都市のグローバリゼーションの状況を浮き彫りにしている。
個展「Path」(台北/2014)、「Find The Center」(台南/2012) 等。

Born in Taipei in 1976, Lai Pei-Yu graduated from the Tainan National University of the Arts Graduate Institute of plastic arts and is currently enrolled in the doctoral program. In her "City Series", she uses dots to underpin the similarities of urban landscape in different locations, and hence highlights the current trend of globalization. Among her recent solo exhibitions are *Path* (Taipei / 2014) and *Find The Center* (Tainan / 2012).

BankART1929での滞在について

BankART1929で制作し、生活した時間は、私の作家としてのキャリアにとってまたとない貴重な経験となりました。作品を創作する努力を継続することと同様、生活体験や視野を拡げることはとても重要なことだと思っています。

この時期、私は都市シリーズの作品制作に取り組んでおり、世界的に有名でありながら、不思議と親しく感じられる都市である横浜で多くを得ることができました。滞在期間中に、展覧会の開催、人々との交流、作品制作上の実験、さらには日本で活動しながら台湾で作品発表できたことなど、多くの大切なことを実現できたことを BankART1929に感謝しております。この交流プログラムで過ごした貴重な時間はずっと私の脳裏に刻まれることでしょう。

賴 珮瑜(2007年3月)

About stay in BankART1929

Spending time at BankArt1929 is an important experience professionally, and also for the development of my artistic creation. The local experience of life and the development of my own vision are similarly important.

During this time I have continued to develop my series of urban work, and have benefited from my visit to this world famous city, which I find strangely familiar. Thanks to the kind assistance of BankArt1929, I have been able to realize many creative aspects of this project: exhibition, exchange, experiment, and presenting the work in Taiwan. My time spent here will remain etched in my mind.

Lai Pei-Yu (March 2007)

「另／原郷」
"Another Homeland"
March 23 — April 8, 2007
BankART Studio NYK／Studio #1

2007
横浜 ⇒ 台北
Yokohama → Taipei

Murata Mineki
村田峰紀

1979年群馬県生まれ。2005年多摩美術大学美術学部彫刻学科卒業。原始的な身体所作で強いインパクトを与えるドローイングパフォーマンスや、その結果として産み出されるインスタレーション、映像等を発表している。

個展、2015年「生PUNK」GALLERY HASHIMOTO(東京)、2014年「ネックライブ」Art Center Ongoing(東京)他。グループ展、2015年「VOCA展2015」上野の森美術館(東京)、2013年「カゼイロノハナ」アーツ前橋(群馬)他。

Born in Gunma prefecture in 1979, Murata graduated from the Sculpture Department at the Tama Art University in 2005. His drawing performances involving primitive gestures have evolved into installation and audio-visual pieces. His solo exhibitions include *Nama Punk* at the Hashimoto Gallery in Tokyo (2015), *Necklive* at Art Center Ongoing, Tokyo (2014). He also participated in the group show *Voca Exhibition 2015* at Tokyo's Ueno Royal Museum and *The Flower with Colour of Wind* at Arts Maebashi (2013).

台北国際芸術村での滞在について

英語をほとんど話せない。日本語もあまり話せないが。

今回の台北滞在がきまり不安な気持ちもあった。しかし言葉を使えないことは、僕の作品にとって大きな影響があると思っていた。伝えきれない内側にある言葉を『ノーコメント』として作品にしてきたからだ。

言葉の通じない、訳のわからない日本人でも作品をつくれば、なんとかなるはずと、信じていた。言葉はしっかり伝わらないが、台湾滞在中に出会った人達と沢山コミュニケーションをとった。文字やドローイング、めちゃくちゃな英語で話した。みんなやさしかった。そして作品は僕の大きな言葉となって語ってくれたと思う。台北で経験した事柄を糧にこれからも、前進していこうと思う。

村田峰紀 (2008年3月)

About the stay in TAV

I don't speak English well, and honestly I am not good at talking with the Japanese language, either. Therefore I was a little nervous when I came to Taipei.

On the other hand, I assumed that the inconvenience in the language would have a positive impact on my work process, as I have being created a series of pieces, called No Comment by consciously using the internal and unutterable words.

I as Japanese don't understand Chinese at all but believed that my work should be able to communicate with people directly.

Though it wasn't with the language, I succeeded to do the communication with people I met during the residency. I wrote letters, made drawings and spoke awful English, then it was so nice to find myself well accepted by people. After all, my work talked a lot for my own words. I think I will work hard and go forward with being encouraged by my experiences in Taipei.

Mineki Murata (March 2008)

グループ展『( )4 =bare 』
1st Season Resident Artists Group Show "( )4 =bare"
29-30 March, 2008
TAV/ 藝術家工作室

2007
台北 ⇒ 横浜
Taipe → Yokohama
Ho Ming-Kuei
何 明桂

1978年嘉義市に生まれる。花蓮師範大学、シェフィールド・ハラム大学卒業。「空間の再創造」というテーマを、リアルなモデルや小道具、想像上の空間を表す特殊なアングルで切り取った写真によって追求している。
個展に「As Dream, As Illusion」(関渡美術館/2014)、「干物女の最終電車」(BankART Studio NYK/2008)。
グループ展「Beyond August 1－Memorial Day」(高雄市立美術館/2015)等に出展。

Born in 1978 Chia-yi city, Ho Ming-Kuei graduated from Sheffield Hallam University and the National Hualien Teacher's College. Working on the "re-creation of space", she pursues the theme with photos representing realistic models, props and imaginary space taken from a special angle. Among her more recent exhibitions are: *As Dream, As Illusion* (Kuandu Museum / 2014), *Himono-onna's Final Call* (BankART Studio NYK / 2008). Group exhibitions include *Beyond August 1-Memorial Day* (Kaohsiung Museum of Fine Arts / 2015).

BankART1929での滞在について

わたしにとっての横浜滞在は、時間のない空間に浮かぶワンダーランドにいるような体験でした。わたしの抱いていた特別な夢が、この2ヶ月間で、期待通り実現した、と思っています。横浜のいろいろな側面を見聞きし、多くの文化的イメージを受け、興味深い人たちとの出会いがありました。 こういった経験を通じて、日本文化のより深い意味に気づき、日本人がどのように世界を認識するかを理解出来たことも、わたしにとっては驚きでした。

横浜に住むことは、西洋と東洋のユニークな混合の中に生きるかのようです。日本のコンテンポラリーアートもこの社会の近代的意味を現しています。さらに、横浜市が街を創造的な場所として再生させようとする努力を続けてきたことはたいへん印象的でした。BankART1929は、空間のエネルギーを持続することに尽力する集団というだけでなく、あらゆる可能性を実現するために常に理想を掲げて、芸術的実践を遂行する人々です。わたし自身も台北の美術館で働くスタッフとして、このような実践に人生を捧げる方たちに、心からの敬意を表したいと思います。ブラボー！

何 明桂 (2008年3月)

About the stay in BankART1929

The life in Yokohama was like a floating wonderland in the timeless space for me. I had a special dream and realized one of my expectations in these two months. Seeing every aspect in Yokohama, I have received many cultural images and met many interesting people there. Through this experience, I therefore understood the deeper meaning of the Japanese culture and realized how Japanese see the world which was as well surprising to me.

Living in Yokohama is as inhabiting with a unique mixture of the west and the east. The contemporary Art in Japan also presents a modern sense of the society. Additionally, the effort of how the Yokohama government has put to promote the city as a creative city site is extremely impressive. BankART1929 was not only a group of people who tried very hard to maintain this energy of the space, but also an art practitioner that presents a constant ideal to realize every possibility. As myself being an art museum staff in Taipei, I truly respect these people who devoted their lives to make things happened. Bravo!

Ho Ming-Kuei (March 2008)

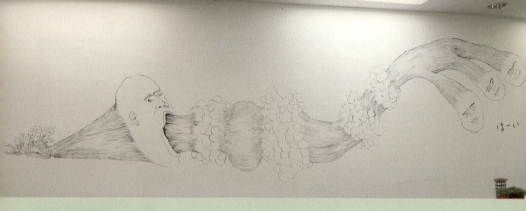

「干物女の最終電車」
"Himono Onna no Saishuu Densha"
23 March- 8 April, 2008
BankART Studio NYK /Studio #1

本当に恐ろしいことを知らないことはオモシロイ?
無知が産み出す諧謔(かいぎゃく)・ユーモア、それが私の作品のテーマです。事件や事故や災害のような非日常的な『経験』は、私たちの生活のまわりに日常的にあふれています。今日、私たちの『経験』はテレビなど様々なメディアの影響を受け、直接体験しないまま私たちの脳裏に刻まれていきます。私のドローイングは、このような『経験』のプロセスを一枚の絵に転写させたものです。それらがドローイングとして外へ複製されるとき、その本質のいくつかは消え去り、かわりにむなしく落ち着かない感覚(ファンタジー)が立ち現れてきます。
今回、横浜での短い滞在の中で、私の頭の中にフラッシュのように生まれてくるイメージを記録していくことを試みました。それらは形のないまま「あれ?」という姿に生まれ変わっていったのです。

何 明桂(2008年3月)

Ignorant humor is the base of my works. Disasters and phenomenon are what we receive in life rather everyday experience. These extraordinary scenes have planted in the non-related audiences and have made impact through broadcasting. My drawings are based on this knowledge. As transforming my fantasy to something visible and tangible, there are always something solid missing and sense fragile through the process of solidification and simulation. Drawing for me is a recording toward the ongoing images around me. Those images from everyday life have been deposited shortly in my mind and reformed on the paper through drawing. Somehow they are distorted with surprise and to illustrate unidentified disorder. They seem to appear as fragments but somehow related to each other underneath. The short stay in Yokohama supplies me such a flash image but somehow they transform to another indescribable state while I am trying to record.

Ho Ming-Kuei (March 2008)

2008
横浜 ⇒ 台北
Yokohama → Taipei

Kawase Kohske
川瀬浩介

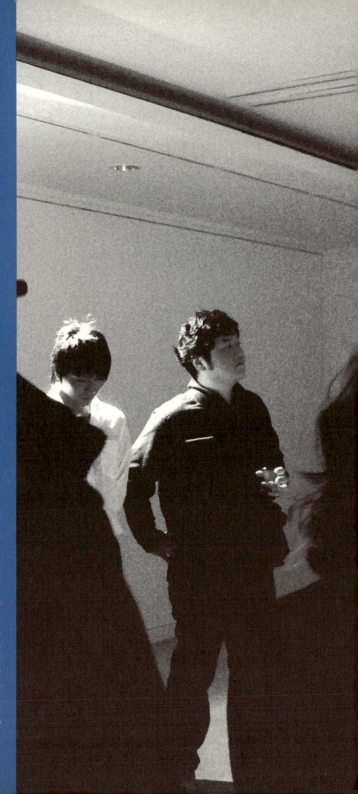

作曲家・美術家。1970年京都生まれ東京育ち。02年、《Long Autumn Sweet Thing》を発表し美術家としてデビュー。10年、第13回文化庁メディア芸術祭に《ベアリング・グロッケンⅡ》が出展。12年、東京スカイツリーにて《光の音色〜a tone of light》を発表。13〜14年、森山開次、ひびのこづえらとの協働によるパフォーマンス《LIVE BONE》が、国内外でツアーを展開。15年には、新国立劇場で行われた森山開次《サーカス》の音楽を担当し、同作品のサウンドトラック《A Small Hope》をリリース。

Born in Kyoto in 1970, Kawase made his artistic debut in 2002 with *Long Autumn Sweet Thing*. In 2010, he exhibited *Bearings Glocken II* at the 13th Arts Council of Japan Media Arts Festival. In 2013-14, in collaboration with Kaiji Moriyama and Kozue Hibino he toured and performed *Live Bone* both at home and abroad. In 2015, he was the musical director for Kaiji Moriyama's *Circus* at the New National Theatre, and released *A Small Hope*, the soundtrack for this piece.

台北での滞在について

「懐かしい感じがするよ」台北に旅立つ前、そんなことを言われた記憶がある。あのとき、何を伝えようとしていたのか？今、振り返ると、その言葉の意味を探すこと…それが僕の旅の目的となっていたようだ。

台北――未来を切り開かんとする最先端の様式と古き良き時代の佇まいを残す街。そこで覚えた最初の肌触りは、何事にも過剰で休む間もないほど加速を続ける僕の日常とは かけ離れたものだった。街は穏やかでいて活気があり、そのうえ人々は、この上ない「過剰なまでの思いやり」を惜しみなく注いでくれる。我々がどこかに置き忘れてしまった大切なものが、今もここには確かに生き続けている。

《なぜ、彼らはこんなにも親切なのか？》台北で必死につかみ取ろうとしたのは、その秘密だ。あいにく、それは今も謎のままだが、ただひとつだけ、わかったことがある。僕がここで覚えた懐かしさは、「優しさ」だった。

川瀬浩介(2009年4月)

About the stay in Taipei

Before embarking on my journey to Taipei I recall being told, "that city evokes 'something'." Now as I look back and analyse what my interlocutor was trying to express, it strikes me that the purpose of my trip was to unearth the meaning of that 'something.'

Taipei is a city where a pioneering spirit reigns, a place in which ancient and contemporary lifestyles comfortably intermingle. My immediate impression upon arrival was to sense something quite distinct from the frenetic nature of my daily life, an existence in which I rarely have the opportunity to sit back and examine the world around me. While Taipei's street life is brisk, a certain calmness nonetheless prevails, and one can't help but notice how exceptionally thoughtful people are. Here, I realized, the Taiwanese have conserved 'something' precious that we in Japan have discarded.

During my stay in Taipei I desperately attempted to unravel the mystery of why people are so kind there. I'm afraid to say that it still remains a puzzle, yet one thing has become manifestly clear: That 'something' evoked in me was none other that kind-heartedness.

KAWASE Kohske (April 2009)

『シーン・オブ・ライト』
"Scene of Light"
27 March - 21 May, 2009
TAV
機材協力：フォステクス　カンパニー

Notes about Scene of Light

All one sees becomes an abstraction when viewed through a camera lens; light, as such, reduces the city's appearance to an idea. 'City Archives' is a sound and light installation series in which visual extracts filmed in a chosen city are reconstructed in conjunction with a soundtrack of live recordings of the cityscape, layered over with original piano music by Kawase Kohske. The 2009 version in the series is an audio-visual tale of two cities: Tokyo and Taipei. The Taipei episode was completed thanks to the Taipei-Yokohama Artist Exchange Program. During his stay in Taipei, Kawase filmed in various symbolic locations throughout the city and its environs: Taipei Station, Night Market, Tanshui, Taipei 101 and elsewhere. The resulting sound and light installation accurately preserved Taipei as it existed in 2009. At the exhibition, the images are projected onto a mirror, in which the spectators can also see a reflection of themselves. Thanks to light, they are encapsulated into the city's images, leading them to engage in a dialogue with their own mental landscapes.

http://www.kawasekohske.info/TAV09/

All that one can see is luminous. You recall being embraced by light.
The light is you. You are luminous.

KAWASE Kohske (October 2009)

シーン・オブ・ライトについて

見るもの全てをカメラのレンズを通して抽象化し、都市の様子を「光」に還元。同時に採取された都市を構成する音と共に映像として再構築した「光と音」による【都市アーカイブ】シリーズ。2009年現在、《東京》《台北》2都市を記録したバージョンが存在する。「台北・横浜アーティスト交換プログラム」の成果として完成した台北バージョンは、現地滞在中に台北駅、夜市、淡水、台北101他、台北とその周辺を象徴するエリアでロケを実施。街で録音されたノイズと自ら奏でたピアノによる音楽と併せて、2009年の台北を「光と音」で完全保存した。展覧会では、映像が鏡に浮かび上がるインスタレーション作品として展開。鑑賞者は、映像と同時に鏡に映る自分自身の姿を見つめ、光として表出された都市の風景に抱かれながら、自らの心象と対話していく。

http://www.kawasekohske.info/TAV09/

目に見えるすべては――光。光に抱かれ、覚えるだろう。
光は、君であることを。君は、光であることを。

川瀬浩介(2009年10月)

2008
台北 ⇒ 横浜
Taipe → Yokohama

Chen Wan-Ling
陳 宛伶

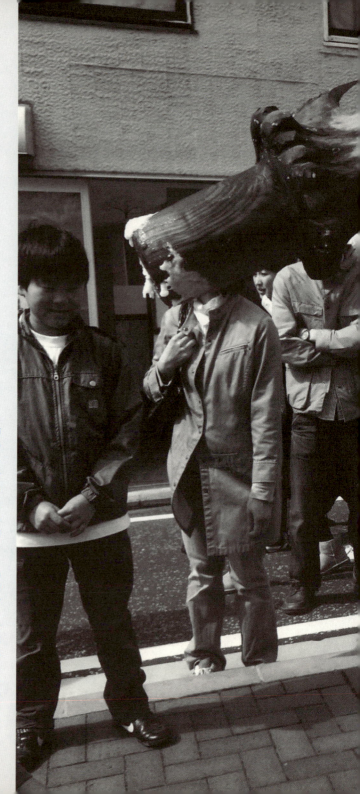

1980年台南に生まれる。現在国立台南芸術大学博士課程に在籍中。横浜のBankART1929とパリのシテ・デ・ザールで滞在制作を行う。現代都市の日常生活への関心に触発された作品づくりを行っている。台湾、香港、中国、韓国、日本、フランス等で作品を発表している。個展に「Micro Nature」(台南/2014)、「陳宛伶展」(パリ/2012)等。

Born in Tainan in 1980, Chen Wan-Ling is currently enrolled at the Tainan National University of the Arts doctoral programme. She participated in residencies at BankART1929 in Yokohama and the Cité des Arts in Paris. She has exhibited in Taiwan, Hong Kong, China, South Korea, Japan and in France. Her most recent solo shows are *Micro Nature* (Tainan / 2014), and *Chen Wan-Ling solo exhibition* (Paris / 2012).

BankART1929での滞在について

私の作品は、つねに都市の生活と密接に関係します。加速の中で静止する身体が、奇妙な視覚的経験を産み出すことから、作品を制作します。横浜滞在中、故郷の台南とは違う都市のなかに住み、一方これまでの創作のコンテクストを継続しながら、新たな生活体験を通じて自分の作品を再考しました。

3ヶ月という短い期間に、「旅」をしたのだと思っています。それは、あちこちに行く旅ではなく、ひとつの所に止まりながら、続いていく旅です。毎日わずかな変化が、私の住まう野毛や制作スタジオにもあります。同様に、異国の生活の緊張やロマンチックな思い、言語上の困難、カルチャーショックもあります。同じアジアの台湾と日本ですが、考え方の違い、生活方式の違いを毎日のように発見しました。また、バンカート1929の友人たちの暖かいもてなしと、たくさんの若いアーティストの作品に接し、とても熱い血を感じました。このような貴重な経験を持てたことを心から幸せに思います。そして、このことは今後の私の創作にとって必ず重要な栄養になると思っています。

陳 宛伶(2009年4月)

Reflections on My Residency at BankART1929

My work is always intimately bound up with city life. It stems from this motionless body existing in a revolving world creating subtle visual experiences. In Yokohama, I had the occasion to live new life experiences, unlike anything I knew in my native Tainan. In some respects what I created in Yokohama was a continuation of what I had previously done, but my experiences here led me to reconsider both my work and my position as an artist. In those 3 short months, I felt as though I had embarked upon a journey; not one in which one travels around the place, but rather a voyage within the bounds of a single location. This journey continued day-in day-out, with every new day bringing a slight change of scenery to my new-found home in Noge and work atelier in BankART Studio NYK. That is not to say that there were not the strains of living in a foreign country, with its foreign language and strange customs. Culture shock occurs when one arrives with idealised notions. Japan and Taiwan are close in geographical terms, yet I witnessed wide differences in many aspects of daily life and in the approach to thinking and speaking. I was truly heartened by my friends at BankART, whose hospitality made me feel at home. With their help I was also able to come into contact with many young Japanese artists. I'm deeply grateful for having been afforded this valuable experience, one which will profoundly nourish me in all my future endeavours.

Chen Wan -Ling (April 2009)

『小宇宙』
"Microcosmos"
12 April - 19 April, 2009
BankART Studio NYK / 2A Gallery

小宇宙について

この一連の作品のはじまりは、私自身が毎日車で通勤していた経験に遡ります。私は、「移動」について思考するようになりました。身体は安全に車両の中に守られており、外の世界はガラスを隔てて、風音、振動が伝わってきますが、直接私自身に繋がってはいません。A地点からB地点に行き、またA地点に戻る。止まっている体がじつは移動していることを、私はどのようにして知るのでしょう。それは、視覚と記号の変化によってのみ、時間の変化と空間の移動を認識するのです。しかしその時、視覚認識と身体感覚は微妙なずれを生じます。

或いは世界の回転があまりに速すぎ、私たちは世界の中心にありながら、自分自身の身体を世界の動きに結びつけることができず、いつもゆっくりと、鈍い反応のなかでしか動けないのかもしれません。しかし、私たちはいつも身辺に回っている一切とひとつの世界を成しています。たとえそれがあまりに速く、遠く、またたとえ私たちが静止したままでいたり、緩慢な動作しかできなくても、いつも私たちは何かを待っているのです。毎日繰り返す出会いの中にすこしずつの変化があり、私たちの指先や視覚の末端から、ついには小宇宙が形成されていくことを。私の作品はそのような小宇宙の描写でありたいのです。

陳 宛伶 (2009年4月)

Microscosmos

I can trace the genesis of this series to the fact that I used to commute by car on a daily basis. This experience led me to contemplate on the whole notion of 'migration' or displacement in space. In a car, we are cocooned from the external world; the windshield acts as a sound-break. Though vaguely aware of the wind and the vibrations of our own bodies, we are, in effect, sealed off from the outside world. In moving from A to B and then back to A again, how can I be sure that I actually moved. All I can rely upon are the various visual stimuli and road-signs that intimate a change in both the hour and the location. At such times, I feel a subtle difference between what my eyes inform me and what my body tells me.

It could well be that the earth is revolving too rapidly: Though we are at its centre, our bodies are incapable of linking with the world around us. Perhaps, our movements or our responses are too slow. And yet, the world we constitute about us is invariably coherent. While it might strike us that we move too quickly, or that the world is too remote from us, or even that our bodies remain motionless, we nonetheless expect that something will occur. The small changes happening in our daily encounters with reality, from the tips of our fingertips to a diversity of physical sensations, ultimately lead to the creation of our individual microcosmos. I can only hope that this series faithfully portrays this microcosmos.

Chen Wan-Ling (April 2009)

2009
横浜 ⇒ 台北
Yokohama → Taipei

Ide Kenji
井出賢嗣

1981年横須賀生まれ。個人、恋愛、生活をテーマに立体インスタレーションで表現をする。近年は物事の裏側にある人間臭い不安定な情緒、センチメンタルな物語を事実、フィクションをない交ぜに制作した立体物とプロセスを示す映像とを合わせて発表している。主な活動、2013年『ノンジャンル(仮)』(アキバタマビ)、『もののやりかた』(＠KCUA)、2012年『井川と白い壁』(Art Center Ongoing)、『about Miss'M』(KUNCI-インドネシア)など。

Born in 1981 in Yokosuka, Ide's installations deal with the individual, love and everyday existence. In recent years, he has explored the all-too-human instable nature of our emotions, producing a mixture which is partially fiction together with visuals that reveal the process. Among his works in 2013 *Non-genre (tentative)* (Akibatamabi); *Mono no yarikata* (@KCUA); *Igawa and White Wall* (Art Center Ongoing) and *about Miss'M* (Kunci - Indonesia) in 2012.

台北での滞在について

2月の初旬、滞在を始めて3週間が経ち、数人の友達ができていた。彼らは親切で、気さくに僕をいろいろなところに連れて行ってくれた。旧正月が近くにあるということもあって、市場や飲食店は賑わい、夜は寺の近くで台湾オペラが行われる。夜市で飯を食べながら、僕はこの国やこの国の人が好きだなと思った。それから時間が経ち、地元の絵画教室に通いながら制作を進めていくうちにその気持ちも膨らんでいった、考えてみれば初めての海外長期滞在だった。僕は初めて自分の国以外のことを肌身に感じていた。そしてそれは恋のような感覚だった。何か気持ちを表せないかと考えた結果、僕はこの国やこの国の人たちにラブレターを送ることにした。まずは僕が彼らを好きだということを理解してもらうために、そして僕のことも好きになってもらうために。僕の恋は始まっている。

井出賢嗣（2010年4月）

About the stay in Taipei

By early February I had already struck up several friendships, some three weeks into my Taipei residency. My friends were open-hearted and so good as to introduce me to various aspects of Taipei's city-life. With Chinese New Years approaching the markets as well as the eating and drinking houses were a bustle with visitors, while the Taipei Opera was performed close to the temple. Over dinner with my new-found friends, it became clear to me that I liked Taiwan and its people. This feeling was only to be all the greater the longer I stayed and as I began attending art classes locally, and becoming more involved with creating new works. Upon reflection, this was my first lengthy overseas stay, and as such the first time I keenly realised differences with my own background and culture. And, this sensation was almost one of love. As a result of not being able to express my feelings, I decided to write a love letter to this country and its people. I first of all wanted them to know that I liked them, and moreover I wanted that they become fond of me. I am beginning to fall in love.

Ide Kenji (April 2010)

『台子に恋してる』
"Falling in love With Taiko"
20 March - 25 April,2010　TAV

台子に恋してる

僕はいま台子に恋してる。彼女はとてもきれいで賢い、そして時々お転婆でとてもお茶目だ。どうにかして彼女をものにしようと手を尽くすけど、彼女は笑うだけでなかなか僕を近づかせない。そんな中、僕は彼女がとても純で、それを愛していることに気がついた。それに気がついてから、僕は彼女を見守ることに決めた。彼女の純情や人の良さを見守るのだ。彼女が生きているだけで僕は幸せだから。活動：私は絵画教室に通いながら、彼女の癖を真似しました。また同時に台湾国内を回りながら彼女のいいところを見つけていきました。この活動の中で徐々に僕は彼女の個性や人間性に気がついていきました。そしてそんな彼女にラブレターを送ることに決めました。つまりこれは思い出ではないのです、今まさに進んでいる気持ちなのです。それが僕の作品です。

井出賢嗣(2010年3月)

Falling in love with Taiko

I'm falling in love with Taiko now. She is beautiful, and smart. Sometimes she is spirited girl. I try to bring around her in some wise. But she only smiles me and she doesn't let me touch. Then I noticed that she is pure. She loves her own pureness. After noticing that, I decided to keep looking her. I save her pureness and her kindness. Her mere existence makes me happy. "Activities" I'm going to painting class in Taipei for borrowing her sign. And I also walk around Taiwan for finding her good part. During these activities, I gradually understand her personality. Then I decided to send love letter to her. It's not a memory. It's ongoing feeling. This is my work.

Ide Kenji (Mach 2010)

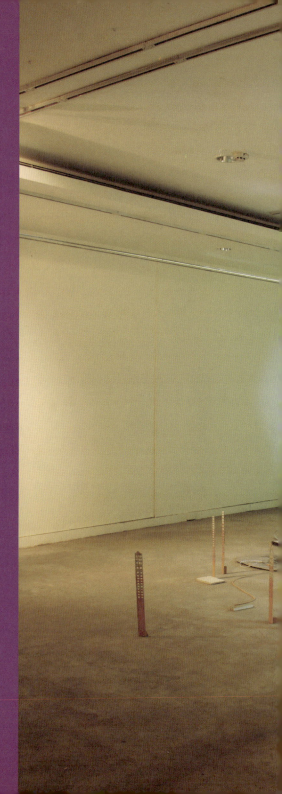

2009
台北 ⇒ 横浜
Taipe → Yokohama

Chou Yu-Cheng
周 育正

1976年台北に生まれる。2007年、パリの国立高等美術学校エコール・デ・ボザール卒業、翌2008年同校のラ・セーヌプログラムに選出される。近年の個展に、「周育正展」(デンバー現代美術館/2008)、「Molyneux」(台北市立美術館/2014)。グループ展に台北ビエンナーレ(台北市立美術館/2012)、「The Great Ephemeral」(New Museum/2015) 他。2012年台北芸術賞グランプリ受賞。

Born in Taipei in 1976, Chou Yu-Cheng graduated from l'Ecole Nationale Supérieure des Beaux-Arts, Paris, in Paris in 2007, and was chosen in 2008 for the La Seine programme. Recent exhibitions include, *Yu-Cheng CHOU* (Denver Museum of Contemporary Art / 2008), *Molyneux* (Taipei Fine Arts Museum/2014). His group exhibitions include: Taipei Biennale (Taipei Fine Arts Museum/2012), *The Great Ephemeral* (New Museum / 2015). He received the Grand Prix at the 2012 Taipei Art awards.

Chou Yu-Cheng 71

Residency Goods
Yu-Cheng CHOU

The Artist Exchange Program 2009 between Taipei and Yokohama
2010.4.17(Sat)-25(Sun)　11:30 -19:00　Opening Party :4.17(Sat) 19:00-

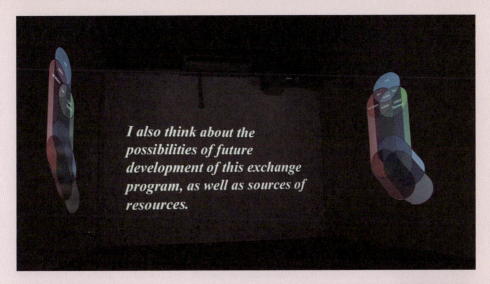

「Residency Goods」
17 April - 25 April, 2010
BankART Studio NYK 2F / Studio201

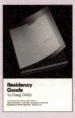

Residency Goods

Residency Goods展は、横浜市台北市アーティスト交流プログラムを前提に進めたプロジェクトです。このなかで、アーティストとしてのわたしが、レジデンス期間中に引き起こされる思考を集積し、一冊の本にまとめます。簡単な言葉を用いてアーティストの存在の事実、ここでの生活やシステムについてのあれこれの話題、またアーティストという立場をごく当たり前と思えるような方法で叙述し描写したいと思います。5年間にわたり続いてきたBankART と TAV の交流事業のなかで、"Residency Goods" を見た方が、この交流についてさらにおおきな想像力と可能性を見い出せるようになれば良いと思います。アーティストである私が、このレジデンスで生み出す成果を展覧会タイトルにある"Goods"として見い出すように。

周 育正（2010年4月）

Residency Goods

The "Residency Goods" is conceived in the actual situation that I myself as an artist am participating in the Yokohama -Taipei Exchange Program. For this exhibition, I collected the ideas caused around the Artist in Residence and described the ongoing program as it was in the very simple words. After all, it came to talking about the daily life here, the system of residency as well as the possible proposals done by the artist.
The exchange between BankART and TAV has run already for 5 years, and I wish that the "Residency Goods" may encourage people to think about the meaning of the exchange and to have better perspectives for its future, just as the goods are created after the productive stay of an artist.

Chou Yu-cheng（April 2010）

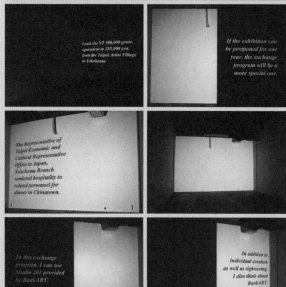

周育正氏とその作品について

周育正氏の作品は、日常生活で経験する、他人にはとるに足らないと思えるような「事件」を表出することから始まります。それらにはプライベートなものからパブリックなものまで、様々な位相のものが含まれています。例えば、子供の頃母親に買ってもらったアメリカ製のクレヨン、台湾の国旗、雑誌やテレビなどのメディアに登場する既存のイメージ等など。周氏は、これらの「素材」をコンピューターを駆使しながら加工し、ドローイングや映像作品のインスタレーションとして表現していきます。

さて今回、BankART studio NYKを中心とした横浜滞在では、「Residency Goods」と題し、レジデンスアーティストとして自らが置かれている状況そのものを題材とし、作品化しました。基本的には文字と図だけからなるインスタレーションと小冊子は、内容的にも表現的にもコンセプチュアルで一見とっつきにくい印象を受けます。しかし、その内容をよくみると「海外でテンポラリーに生活し、作品をつくる」という「異邦人」として経験する様々な事象／空間／関係を、極めて自然にテーマ化し、誠実に反応した作品といえるでしょう。例えば作品の文中に登場する『作品を発表したあとは、すぐにレジデンスしていた町を離れる』などのセンテンスは、極あたりまえのことを記しているだけなのですが、レジデンスプログラムそのものについて「意味と限界」を改めて考えさせてくれます。前出の母親からもらったクレヨンをテーマした作品も、決して思い出の品のようなとり扱いはせず、写真を大きく引き延ばしライトボックス化し、まるで「看板広告」のようなクールな表現方法がとられています。このように、彼は自身を取り巻く状況に対して一定の距離をとること、すなわち、自己の位置／場所の相対化と俯瞰的な視座の獲得こそが、彼の表現のベースといえるでしょう。強いプライベートな思い入れも、パブリックなレギュレーションも、常に冷静な目で、同じパースペクティブで、その確かさを捉えたいという周氏の真摯な意志、あるいは疑うことと信じることを繰り返すことで不確かさをそぎ落としていこうとする行為、その作業そのものが、彼の作品の制作の方法であり、またその作品そのものであるといえるでしょう。

BankART1929

Yu-Cheng Chou: The Artist and his Works

Seen from the perspective of everyday life, the starting point for Taiwanese artist Yu-Cheng Chou's works might strike onlookers as inconsequential given that his exhibits could almost be considered as non-events. Embracing objects from both private and public spheres, Chou's works incorporate traces of his multi-phased existence. Childhood memories, for instance, are evident in Because 64 Crayons Made in the USA, (2009) a box of coloured crayons his mother gave to him as a child. Juxtaposing such diverse objects as a Taiwanese flag with sundry images from the print, TV and various other new media, he offers a virtual compendium of contemporary artistic practice. Chou freely avails of these 'raw materials', processing them with the aid of computers, and subsequently re-assembling them as installations featuring drawings and audio-visual works.

Residency Goods, a project initiated as part of an artists residency exchange-program between Yokohama's BankART1929 and AIR Taipei in which Chou compiled his experiences in the form of a booklet and an installation. BankART Studio NYK showcases Chou's works, principally consisting of drawings and written statements, conceived and created during his residency. The installation's title, Residency Goods, refers specifically to the works created in-situ. At first sight, Chou's works might come across as somewhat inaccessible, given the conceptual nature of their content and expression. On closer scrutiny, however, it becomes clear that they are nothing less than the embodiment of his direct experience, that of an outsider temporarily resident overseas. Thematically, they embrace in the most natural way possible, the various images/ spaces/ relationships he confronts during his sojourn, and can be understood as a direct response to his sense of de-placement. A telling example is a text extract featured in one of the works on display: "The artists shall leave the stationed residency when his new work is published." While it might strike one as a self-evident utterance, he induces one to reflect over the actual significance and limits of the residency programme itself.

Even the previously mentioned Because 64 Crayons Made in the USA is by no means presented as a memento; he transforms this erstwhile plaything into an object of display: the ensuing images no longer represent childhood. Through effective use of enlarged photos, digital processing and Light-box scripts, his works are billboard-like, exemplifying a sophisticated contemporary graphic sense. In this way he maintains a certain distance from the situation he finds himself in. His aesthetic credo entails him confronting and acquiring an overview of his position/location. Whether dealing with an expansive private world, or public entertainment, he invariably approaches his material with a detached eye. Chou's determination to earnestly endeavour to grasp the notion of certitude, or alternatively his constant reiteration of doubts and beliefs, underlie his efforts to grapple with uncertainty. While forming the basis for his output, this work process in itself constitutes a work-of-art.

BankART1929

2010
横浜 ⇒ 台北
Yokohama → Taipei

Isaji Yugo
伊佐治雄悟

1985年岐阜県に生まれる。多摩美術大学を卒業後、関東を中心に活動。様々な技法を用いて、ボールペンやホッチキスなどの日用品を素材とした作品を制作する。近年には、これまでの台北、台中、横浜／黄金町でのレジデンスの経験や交流を生かして、国内外で活動の幅を広げている。

Born in 1985 in Gifu Prefecture, Isaji graduated from the Tama Art University. Using a variety of techniques his artworks incorporate materials such as a ballpoint pens and staplers. He avails of his wide experience of cultural exchanges in Taiwan and Yokohama to expand upon his range of activities.

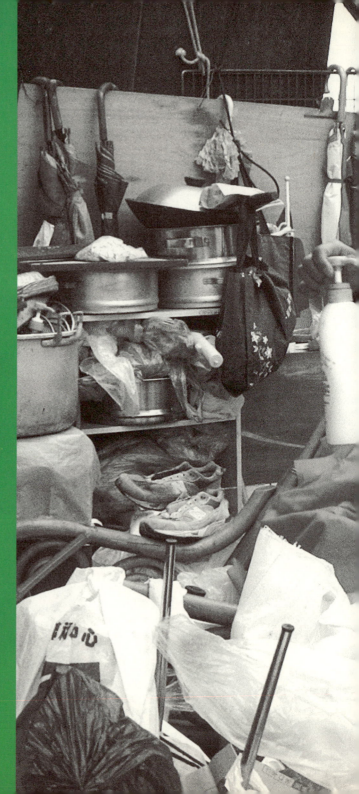

TAVでの展覧会・ワークショップ・THAV住民との交流

滞在中、TAVに滞在している作家による展覧会に参加し、滞在中に制作した新作を発表しました。TAVでの制作は、スペースの広いスタジオや、台北駅近くの良い環境に恵まれていました。こういったレジデンス環境があったことで普段以上に制作に集中でき、作品のクオリティを求めることができました。

またTAVでは施設の教室を利用して一般の参加者と一緒に、私が用意したものに加えて、要らなくなった玩具を集めて、「前よりもいい玩具を造る」ワークショップを企画しました。私が普段制作に使用しているグルーガンなどの工具を参加者に使ってもらいました。TAVでは、アートに限らず、頻繁にダンス、演劇等のワークショップや教室が催されています。なので、私のワークショップの参加者もTAVのことをよく知っており、気軽に参加して楽しんでもらえたようです。ワークショプ終了後には完成した作品は、(責任をもって)持ち帰ってもらいました。

THAVでは、住人の協力を得て不要品を作品にするプロジェクトを行いました。THAVの住人の多くは中国から兵士として渡って来た現在では高齢の方々です。ここでは毎日一世帯ずつ、福祉団体の方が郵便を届けがてら、そうしたご老人の様子を見て回っています。私は彼らに同行することで、不要品を受け取りました。この仕事はレジデンス期間中の最初のものですが、「(世界中)どこででも手に入るもので作品をつくる」ことを前提としている私にとっては必要なリサーチでした。なので、このプロジェクトはこの台北でのレジデンスに限らず、今後あらゆる場所で活動を続けて行く上で作家としての私の糧になるものでした。

伊佐治雄悟(2011年4月)

Exhibition and Workshop at TAV; Interaction with local residents in THAV

During my residency at TAV, I participated in exhibitions organized by the other artists-in-residence, while also creating new works. For the production of my new works, I benefited from the large studio space at TAV and the exceptionally suited environment close to Taipei railway station. Thanks to such ideal working-conditions, I could focus on creating works of unusually high quality. Moreover, TAV organized a workshop for the general public in one of their classroom facilities entitled, " More so than in the past Toys are well-made nowadays, " for which I collected toys that were no longer being used, along with some materials and tools I had assembled beforehand. I had participants use the glue-gun I work with on a daily basis. Activities at TAV are not strictly limited to the fine arts, but frequently embrace theatre and dance workshops. Those who participated in my workshop were well aware of TAV's programs, and felt relaxed about joining in and having some fun. After the workshop I had the participants take home the works they had completed, entrusting them with their safe-keep.With the assistance of local residents, the Treasure Hill Artist's Village (THAV) co-ordinated a project in which I created a new piece from various dispensable or discarded items. The majority of THAV residents are former military personnel and soldiers, who crossed over from the mainland, forming as such an elderly community group. Personnel from a local welfare organization visit each of the households in the area every day to deliver the post, and so keep an eye on how the elderly individuals are getting along. I joined the 'postman' on his daily round and was thus able to collect materials required for the project. I undertook this work during the initial stages of my residency, for I assumed that "the materials required for creating an artwork are at hand anywhere in the world," yet in effect this footwork was an indispensable step in bringing the project to fruition. Consequently, this project undertaken during my residency in Taipei not only served as a source of inspiration for me as an artist there, but will continue to do so wherever I happen to be henceforth.

Isaji Yugo (April 2011)

オープンスタジオ

TAVでは作家が滞在している部屋の一般公開を定期的に行っています。スタジオには作家の生活スペースも含まれている為か、お茶を飲んだりしながら作家と話をしたりと、どこかリラックスした雰囲気が漂っていました。

作家の滞在の日程によっては、オープンスタジオの準備時間は限られます。追いつめられたアーティストは各々、それを乗り越えるアイディアを発揮します。私は、与えられたとても広いスタジオの空間を扱うのに苦心しましたが、あえて部屋の中心に小さな作品を展示し、来場者の視点を集中させるように工夫しました。「部屋の広さの割には作品が小さい」という問題を克服したのです。このような環境で、作家がキッチンやソファの隣に作品を展示しながら、何を最優先にしているのかを伺う事が出来ます。この機会は、まさに「オープンスタジオ」と呼ぶに相応しいものでした。

伊佐治雄悟（2011年4月）

Open Studio

The Taipei Artist's Village （TAV） have launched an interactive-forum whereby the artist-in-residence opens up their studio to the general public on a regular basis. Since the studio also contains the artists' living quarters, visitors can converse with them face to face in a homely atmosphere over a cup of tea. Preparation time for the open studio is naturally limited. Artists respond to this challenge individually, each displaying an original approach as to how to overcome the constraints of limited time and space in which to exhibit their works. While I personally struggled to come to grips with the vast studio space, I deliberately placed a small-sized artwork in the middle of my living environment so as to focus my visitors' regard. This enabled me to draw attention to the problem of displaying " a small-sized work in a relatively large room." In fact, such an environment - where works are displayed beside a sofa or in the kitchen - enables one to question their intrinsic worth, and view them in context. "Open studio" sums up the process perfectly.

Isaji Yugo (April 2011)

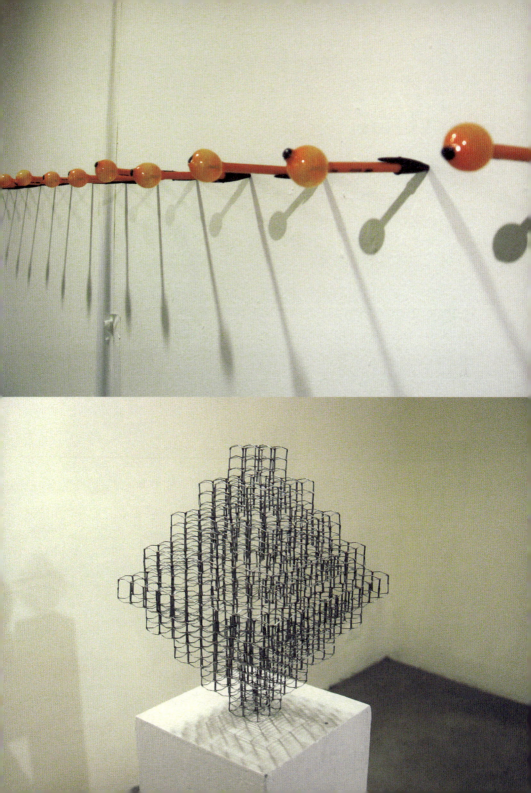

2010
台北 ⇒ 横浜
Taipe → Yokohama
Chen Yi-Huei
陳 怡慧

作曲家、ピアニスト。ロンドンのミドルセックス大学作曲科修士課程卒業。ピアノ演奏と様々なパフォーミングアーツを結びつける作品づくりでよく知られている。伝統音楽、サウンドアート、現代音楽の各分野において、独自の音楽的解釈を駆使しながら、慣習的なコンセプトを打ち破り、音楽の持つ潜在的な可能性を探求している。

Composer and pianist, Chen Yi-Huei received her Master's Degree in Composition from the Middlesex University London. She is well-known for creating works that combine piano performance with various performing arts. Chen has crashed through the pre-existing conventionalized concept in search of the potential musical elements in the fields of traditional music, sound art and modern music.

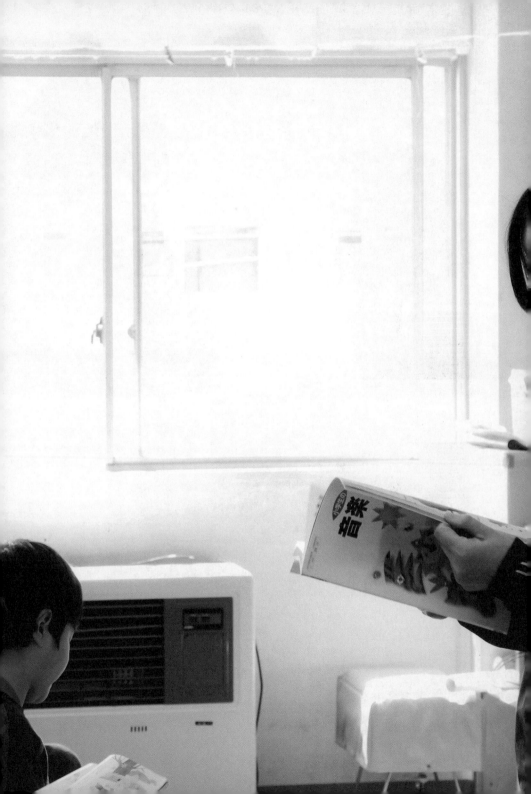

「Inter_Face」
26 August, 2011
Shin Minato-mura

音が交わされ、流れていくなか、記憶に残るものは何か？
光をたどるように、あるルートを通って音の原点にさかのぼる、時折そうせざるを得ない場合もある。うるさい指示音や騒音、轟音の中、その原点が切り離され、静寂が現れる。あるいは、別の方法で、騒ぎはいつかかき消されていく。全ての音は静まり、そして再びよみがえり…
2011年BankARTのレジデンスプログラムで、生活環境を取り巻く音に様々な方法で触れてみるプロジェクトを行なった。それらの音は、環境空間を構成するだけでなく、私達の生活をも構築している。写真がそうであるように、音声も、一人一人にとって意味の異なる表象になり得る。BankARTスタジオでの日常音と東小学校の子供たちの音声を録った二種類の素材は、収集した音とライブピアノ演奏を通してひとつのイメージになる。過去の時を振り返ってみるように、現在つくり出している音も過去のものになっていく。

陳 怡慧（2011年8月）

What's left in our memory with the exchange and flowing of sound?
As the light, we can trace back the sound origin in certain route when sometimes we just have to.
It is separated within the noisy order, disturbance and rumbling sounds, then, still emerges. Or, in another way, the disturbance will be muted someday.
All the sound calms down and returns again...
The project I did my residency of Bankart in 2011 was that I tried to touch the sound around my living environment in different ways. Those sounds construct the environment space and also our life. As photos, sounds/voices could be the symbol with different meanings for different individuals. Two groups of recorded materials, which include daily sounds in Bankart Studio NYK and sounds/voices from Azuma elementary school kids, will turn out to be one image through the interpretation of live piano performance with those collected sounds. Just like looking back at the past time, the sounds crated at present will be the past ones.

Chen Yi-Huei (August 2011)

作曲家ChenYi-huei（チェン・イーホェイ）の滞在制作プランは、日本での身近な生活空間で採集した音と、自身が作曲した（する）ピアノの楽曲を重ね合わせてライブパフォーマンスをおこなうというもの。来日してすぐに彼女は、スタジオのあるBankART Studio NYKの施設内や、居住しているBankARTかもめ荘からNYKまでの往来から、丁寧に日常の音声をピックアップしていく作業に着手しました。また横浜市立東小学校に協力をいただき、音楽の授業やホームルームの時間から、特別な音声もピックアップすることができました。ところが滞在も終盤にさしかかろうという3月11日に東日本大震災が勃発。諸事情でやむを得ず制作の継続を断念し、急遽帰国ということになりました。既に季節は初春から真夏に変わっていましたが、彼女の強い希望で、横浜トリエンナーレ2011と特別連携したBankART1929の企画「新・港村」のプログラムの中で再来日を果たしました。そして、入念にプラクティス、リハーサルを繰り返し、新・港村ホールでの成果発表では、150人以上の観客を動員するという、オープンスタジオの域を超えた本格的なコンサートでファイナルを飾ることができました。

BankART1929

During her stay in Japan, the Taiwanese artist and composer Chen Yi-huei continually worked with soundscapes, making field recordings, collecting sound samples from her daily environment, mixing

them with pieces she composed for piano with the ultimate aim of performing them for a live audience. Right after her arrival in Japan, Yi-huei started carefully recording sounds she came across in the course of her daily commute between her residency studio at BankART Kamome-so and BankART Studio NYK, as well as those encountered within Studio NYK building. With the assistance of the Yokohama Azuma elementary school, she was able to record some particular sounds during music lessons and home-room classes.

The March 11th earthquake and tsunami struck just as she was about to enter the final phase of preparation. Having to abandon the work-in-process, she made a hasty departure to Taiwan. In due course the season changed from early spring to high-summer, and with it her ardent desire to return to Yokohama was fulfilled when she participated in the Shin Minato-mura at the 2011 Yokohama Triennale, part of the special program produced by BankART1929. After repeatedly rehearsing with scrupulous care at the venue, the fruits of her endeavors culminated with a complete concert program, going far beyond the constraints of an open-studio experiment, drawing an audience of 150 to the Shin Minato-mura hall.

BankART1929

2011
横浜 ⇒ 台北
Yokohama → Taipei

Koda Chie
幸田千依

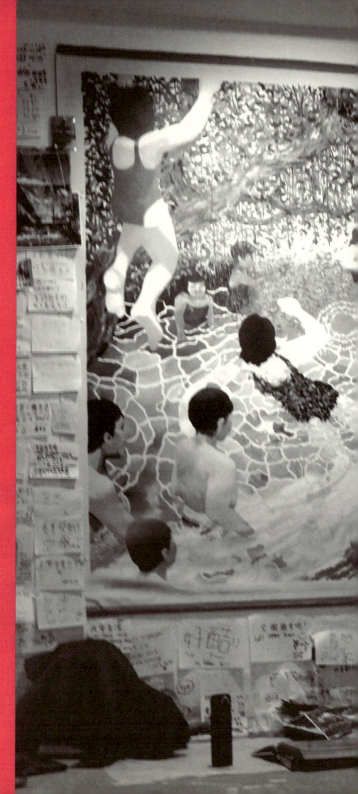

1983年東京生まれ。2007年多摩美術大学卒業。様々な場所に住みながらつくる滞在制作を中心とした活動を行っている。完成した絵画を展示するだけでなく、公開制作を自覚的に行うなど、自身が絵画をつくる過程を見せること、人と作品との出会い方について考え、描くことと見せることの両方について模索。「歩く絵の冒険」など、絵画を室内以外で見せる試み等も展開中。

Born in Tokyo in 1983, Koda graduated from the Tama Art University in 2007. Living in various locations, she has to date focused on creating works in-situ. In addition to un-finished paintings, she has deliberately explored painting with the public present. She addresses the process both in terms of painting and showing the artwork. Among the works currently on exhibit is *The Adventures of a Walking Picture*, with which she is seeking to find alternative exhibition spaces to the indoor art gallery.

歩く絵のパレード in 台北

A Walking Pictureman Paradeは、絵画が人の日常に飛び込んで行くということです。それは近年私が、自分の制作を公開したりすることの意味と関係していて、芸術というものや芸術家の非日常の行為というものを、人の日常の時間や風景の中にゆっくりと時間をかけて浸透させていきたいという思いから発しています。「歩く絵君」は、私の意志が街へ飛び出した結果だと思っています。

日常の空間で絵をみる不思議！
そこでは確かに、絵画は二次元という状態を越えて、ものとしての存在感を表します。しかし、それと同時に強く思ったのは、濃い緑の樹やざらざらした壁や空や人と、絵画が絶妙になじんでその風景がとても輝いたということでした。目にうつる全部の空間が芸術のようでした。台北に住む人にとっては見慣れたいつもの街が、絵画の作用によってもう一度新しく光を放つことを願って、パレードをしました。このパレードのサブタイトルは「Let's Play Around the Picture!」です。これは、最初の公開制作のときに絵の周りでみなで遊んだ経験からつけたタイトルです。パレードでもまさにこのタイトル通り、絵の周りでみなが遊び、笑い、知らないひと同士が出会うのを見ました。それは私にとってとても嬉しいことでした。この経験を忘れません。

幸田千依（2012年4月）

A Walking Pictureman Parade in Taipei

A Walking Pictureman Parade is a series of paintings that encounters everyday existence, by literally taking them to the streets. Closely connected with the meaning and relevance of my works in recent years, they originated from the desire to quietly permeate the lives of ordinary everyday people with the extraordinary world of art and artists. Consequently, I feel as though this series embodies my determination, by bursting into the lives of those walking the city streets. What a strange sight to see these paintings amongst everyday objects in the streetscape!

These paintings surpass two-dimensional representation; they actually reveal life's presence. It strikes me at the same time that these landscapes' exquisitely capture the resplendently dark-green foliage, the rough-hewn walls, the skies and those human figures beneath it. All the eye observes has an artistic quality. I painted this series in the hope that it would enable the people of Taipei to look at their native city they know so well in a fresh light. Their sub-title is: Let's Play Around the Picture! I added this sub-title on remarking the cheerful response of all those exposed to the paintings for the first time. As the title suggests, I observed how everybody responded with laughter and gaiety, and how it created a sense of solidarity among its viewers. It was such an unforgettable experience for me; one that made me extremely happy.

Koda Chie (April 2012)

オープンスタジオ

Taipei Artist Villageでは、2月4日〜3月18日のあいだ、TAVの一階のギャラリーで毎日朝から夜まで一枚の絵を描き続け、そのプロセスを公開しました。毎日沢山の台湾の人や外国の人に出会い、様々な話を、絵の前ですることができました。私は中国語を話すことができません。だからこそ、知りたい！ それをコミュニケーションの糸口にしたい！と思い、絵の前で出会った人たちに「あなたの大切な中国語(台湾語)を教えてください」と尋ねていました。台湾の人は本当にとても優しい！ 皆が、思い思いの言葉を教えてくれました。私は毎日沢山の人に出会い、新しいことを覚え、変わっていきました。私の描く絵も、日々変わっていきました。絵を描きながら、この絵がどういうものになれば良いかを考えていました。台湾の人はみな本当にオープンマインドで、例えばひとりの人がわたしにお菓子をくれて それを食べながら話していると、そこにまたひとり別の訪問者がやってきて、今度はそのふたりが喋りだす。そこにまた新しい人が加わって…笑ってる。

私は中国語がほとんどわからないけれど、とても楽しそうに色々な人がこの絵の前で出会って話したり一緒に遊んだりするのを見ていました。私の絵の中には、台湾の印象的な木である、榕樹の木が描かれています。東京と非常に似ている台北の景色の中で、この榕樹の木がとても際立ちます。台湾の人にとっては、この木はどこにでもあるありふれたものかと思いますが、私はこの樹の存在感がとても好きです。だから、これを絵に描きいれました。はじめはそこまで深い意味を考えて描いたわけではないのですが、絵を描くにつれ、台北で暮らすにつれ、この絵が樹そのもののように思えてきました。大きな樹の下で沢山の人が集い、話し、遊ぶような、この樹の下でたくさんのエピソードが生まれるような、そんな絵を描きたいと思うようになりました。今、この絵を見ていると、絵の前で出会った人のことや話したこと、教えてもらった中国語や遊びの風景が一度に思い出されます。絵画の良いところは「終わらない」ということです。過去も未来も現在もその一枚に含みこんで、いつもそこにあるということです。人によって絵画の作用は様々ですが、見よう、と思うことで絵画は、いつでも見ることができます。絵画を継続的に見ることで、そこに日々を重ねて見ていくことができます。たくさんの台湾の人が、この絵の制作過程を何度も見てくれました。一枚の平面の絵画の中に、何層もの思い、記憶、イメージが重なって厚みを持ったらいいなあと思っています。

幸田千依 (2012年4月)

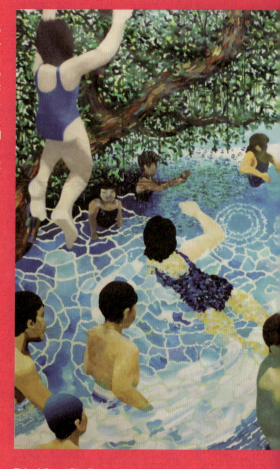

Taipei Open Studio
From morning till evening from February 4th until March 18th, I continually worked on a painting in the presence of the public in the gallery of the 1st floor at the Taipei Artist's Village. This enabled me to meet and talk with many Taiwanese and foreign visitors on a daily basis right in front of my work. Given that I cannot speak Chinese, I wanted to communicate with those around me and availed of this occasion as a means of initiating contact. I asked the studio visitors: "Please teach me a Taiwanese or Chinese word, whatever is close to your heart." The Taiwanese are so friendly that they gladly taught me various phrases and words. During my Taiwanese sojourn I met many people, learnt a lot new things, while in the process undergoing a transformation myself. My work also gradually changed. While painting the series, I kept wondering how they would eventually turn out. Given that the people of Taipei are truly open-minded, I had many positive encounters with the locals.

One of them brought me cakes, which we enjoyed together while talking. Another visitor then dropped by, and they in turn started talking to each other. And someone else came along and joined in the conversation....all in all it was such an enjoyable experience.

Though my knowledge of Chinese is next to nothing, I could nonetheless observe how people responded so positively and with joy on meeting each other around these paintings that often depict that most impressive of native Taiwanese trees, the Chinese Banyan. It is truly an outstanding specimen even in a Taipei setting - whose scenery closely resembles Tokyo. While the locals might take the Banyan for granted, assuming it grows everywhere, I was particularly fond of its expansive character. That was what inspired me to start working on this series. Though initially I didn't attach any particular significance to them, during the process of painting itself and settling in to Taipei life, they became to embody nature of the tree itself. And like the shadow of this overarching tree, they offered the public a place in which they could gather, talk and play with each other, thus becoming the setting for many a human episode. This inspired me even further to continue with the series. Now, as I look at the paintings all that occurred in their presence comes to mind: all those I met, the different stories I heard, the various Chinese phrases I picked up, the laughter and fun.

The good thing about the painting is that it 'never ends.' At once embracing past, present and future; it has a constant quality to it. While approaches may vary towards the process itself, one can look at the work at any time, if ever the mood strikes. One realises by continually watching the work in progress, as did the many onlookers who observed the process in Taipei that one can keep looking at them day after day. I hope that from within the depths of the multi-layered strata of these works memories, desires and images might surface.

Koda Chie (April 2012)

2011
台北 ⇒ 横浜
Taipe → Yokohama

Lo Shih-Tung
羅 仕東

国立台南芸術大学造形美術大学院卒業後、キュレーター、アーティストとして活動。アジアの記憶とコミュニティとの対話にフォーカスしながら、忘れられた歴史を回復する仕事等に取り組んでいる。2011年ポンピドーセンターで「Rencontres Internationales Paris/Berlin/Madrid」に出展。台湾のアーティストが自主運営する「オープンコンテンポラリーアートセンター」のディレクターを務めた。

After graduating from the Tainan National University of the Arts Plastic Arts Institute Lo Shih-Tung became active as a curator and artist. Focusing on Asian memory and the sense of community, he is striving to recover the continent's forgotten history. In 2011, he exhibited at the "Rencontres Internationales Paris / Berlin / Madrid" at the Pompidou Center. He was appointed director of Open-Contemporary Art Center, a Taiwanese contemporary art space run by an artists' collective.

滞在について

BankART Studio NYKでのレジデンス体験は、私にとっては、単にひとつのスタジオ、或いはアートスペースにレジデンスするということではなかった。むしろそれは、横浜という都市そのものの中でのレジデンスであったとおもう。いやもっと明確に、しかしまたぼんやりとではあるが、それは横浜という都市の隙間に入り込む体験だったと思う。かもめ荘のある旧市街区からバンカートのある都心部までを歩く道のり、高層ビルと低層住宅、過去と現在の間にある隙間を流れ動きながら、今まさに未来に向かおうとする横浜という都市と、その郷愁を読み取り、感じていたのだった。

羅 仕東(2012年4月)

BankART Residency

My experience of the residency at Yokohama's BankART Studio NYK was not merely one of having a studio and art space at my disposal, but one of being a resident of the city itself. While somewhat vague, I still had the distinct impression of experiencing what it is like to get to know Yokohama from the inside. Strolling from Kamome-so as far as BankART, from the residency studio located in one of the city's older quarters to the ultra modern downtown district, I walked between the city's past and present, between low- and high-rise, all the while sensing a city striving towards the future and yet suffused with a particular nostalgia.

Lo Shih-Tung (April 2012)

「ドン・キホーテは誰だ？」
Who is Don Quixote?
March 16 – 31, 2012
BankART Studio NYK／Studio201

私は物語を語ることが好きです。また物語を理解することも好きです。物語の内容を語ると言うだけでなく、その物語がどのように語られ、誰が語るのか、いろいろな角度から一つの物語を見るのが好きです。横浜に滞在している間、漢字言語の相似性や日本が台湾を統治していた時代に持ち込まれた生活のディテールの似よりに気づいた以外に、現在の台湾の消費トレンドとB級カルチャーのプロトタイプに行き当たることができました。それは、現実感のある日常領域に属しているのですが、ミシェル・フーコーの提起するヘテロトピアのように、現実と想像の両者が混在する社会のパッチワークの中にあります。なかでも、総合ディスカウントストアのドン・キホーテは私の好奇心をそそるものでした。それは、様々の商品を取り揃え安い価格で販売する生活用品のスーパーマーケットです。「ドン・キホーテ」という名称をスペイン文学の古典から引用していますが、一方でそのレイアウトはけばけばしく、見かけはとても大げさに見えます。寓話と現実の間に大きな対比と緊張関係があります。これは結局笑って済ますことなのか、あるいは現代の寓話なのか。「徹底抗戦」、「安売りへの挑戦」といったスローガンは、私たちの生活に新たな想像を生み出すのか。人と人の関係を作り上げるのか、壊しているのか。この「ドン・キホーテ」は一体誰なのでしょう。どこにいて、何をしているのでしょう。このたびの観察を通して、創作に向かう私のなかで、終わることのない問いかけがはじまったのです。

羅 仕東（2012年3月）

Not only do I enjoy to telling stories, I also like to understand what they are about. It's not simply a case of delivering the story's content or how best to narrate it or even of who tells it but of examining it from various angles. While staying in Yokohama I was able to observe the striking similarities in the kanji or Chinese characters used in Japan and Taiwan, along with the various life-style details still prevalent in Taiwan from the time it was under Japanese rule. In addition, I came across the prototypes for the prevailing trends in Taiwan's popular culture. While belonging to the realm of the everyday, as postulated in Michel Foucault's notion of Heterotopia, this social patchwork embraces both real and imaginary aspects. What particularly intrigued me in the midst of all this was the ubiquitous presence of the Don Quixote stores, a discount retail chain which stocks a variety of household items at bargain prices. Borrowing its name from Cervantes' masterpiece, the store's layout was not only flamboyant but deliberately over the top. A strikingly stark contrast exists between the fable and the reality. I had to question myself whether it is a modern fable, or merely a laughing matter. Do such promotional slogans engender a new imaginary force in our lives? Or, do they forge or destroy relationships between people: Who really is this 'Don Quixote'? Where on earth is he and what is he doing? Thanks to such observations during my stay in Yokohama, I could re-approach my creative process, tackling afresh such interminable questions.

Lo Shih-Tung (March 2012)

2012
横浜 ⇒ 台北
Yokohama → Taipei
Matsuda Naoki
松田直樹

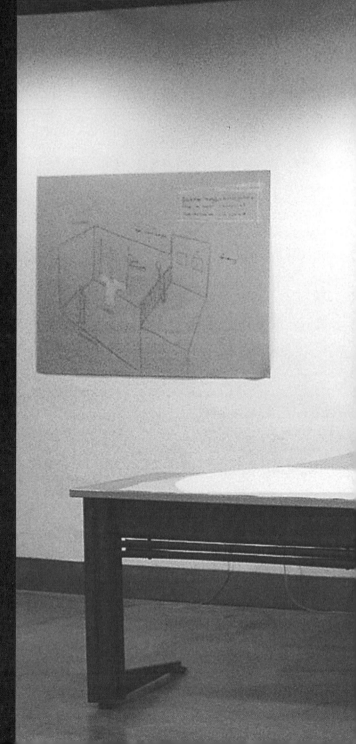

1983年生まれ。2009年東京芸術大学大学院修了。米、髪の毛、埃、指紋、血液、納豆など様々な素材を使った作品を制作。「エプロン」が第7回SICFグランプリ、卒業制作「ヘア・ドレス」が大学美術館の買い上げ賞を獲得。
主な個展に、10daysセレクション - 予兆のかたち10 - (INAXギャラリー2)、BankART Bank under 35(BankART Mini Gallery)など。

Born in 1983, Matsuda graduated from the Tokyo University of the Arts postgraduate course in 2009. Rice, hair, dust, fingerprints, blood, natto are but some of the materials he uses. With *Apron* he was awarded the 7th SICF Grand Prix. He has participated in the BankART Bank under 35 at the BankART Mini Gallery and exhibited at *the 10-days selection - a sign in the form of 10 -* at the INAX Gallery 2.

TAVでの滞在について

「台北で自分の代表作のひとつになるような作品をつくる」というのをこの滞在の一番の目的と決めていました。今の自分にとってこれは最も重要なことです。なぜなら、大学を卒業して数年間、この3ヶ月のような環境を日本でつくるのは困難でした。TAVでは、場所のこと、お金のこと、時間のことを気にせずに制作でき、しかも、たくさんの出会いがあります。

例えば、もう1つのアーティストビレッジであるTHAV (Treasure Hill Artist Village) との交流です。鍋を囲みながら自分の作品について話す会、お互いのアトリエを訪問する会、地元のアーティストのオススメスポットに出かける会... 国が違うと反応も様々ですが、アーティスト同士だからこそ、共感できる部分も多いです。公式のオープンスタジオでは、2日間の日程でそれぞれのアーティストに1人ずつボランティアの通訳が付いてくれました。ボランティアの方は、私の制作を解説する為に、積極的に作品を理解しようとしてくれていたのが印象的でした。毎週末にはTAVカフェでパーティーも開催されます。そこでは、台湾で活躍しているアーティストと知り合いになり、ギャラリーを案内してもらったり、台湾のアートのことについて教えてもらいました。そして、一番印象深いのが樹火博物館の人たちとの出会いです。滞在しているアーティストの勧めで訪れ、今回の作品の支持体になる紙を売っていただきました。その後、私の展示や作品集を見て、紙美術館の方から連絡をいただき、再度、樹火博物館を訪れました。2時間近く、館長を始めとする数人の方と話をして、将来的に展覧会を一緒に作ろうということになりました。実現するかはわかりませんが、展示をして、こういった反応があるのはとてもうれしいことです。　振り返ってみると、恐らく100人近くの方に、自己紹介をしています。こんな状況は、日本にいたら考えられません。多くの出会いをしながらの制作は、常に頭の中をフレッシュに保つことができる貴重な時間でした。

松田直樹 (2013年4月)

About my residency at Taipei Artist Village

The major objective I set out for myself on embarking on this residency at TAV was to create an important body of work. At this stage of my development as an artist, this represents a vital step. Following graduation I wanted to achieve something and these short three months in Taipei provided the ideal occasion - as creating such a productive working environment had been problematic in Japan. The residency in TAV finally afforded me the opportunity to concentrate on my work without being hassled by deadlines or financial constraints, and moreover enabled me to chance upon others who were receptive of my work.

One such example was the exchange with artists at THAV (Treasure Hill Artist Village). Over a meal I was able to discuss my works and later visit the other local artists' ateliers and nearby hot spots they recommended. While each society naturally has its own particular way of interacting with visitors, the fact is that we all share one thing in common, namely, being an artist, and this often led to fruitful exchanges. For the official opening, a volunteer interpreter was assigned to each artist for the 2 days. I was impressed at how conscientious the interpreters were in trying to understand the artists' works so that they could explain them properly to the public.

Each weekend TAV holds a part at its café. There I was able to come into contact with Taiwanese artists and gallery owners, and to learn more about the local art scene. The most important meeting for me, however, was with the staff of the Suho Memorial Paper Museum. I visited them upon the recommendation of a fellow residency artist. I purchased paper there used as the basis for my present creation. They subsequently came to visit my exhibition, and I was at a later stage re-contacted by the Paper Museum. On visiting the museum once again, I spoke at first directly with the director of the museum - and later with other staff members - for some two hours concerning a future exhibition of my work at the museum. Whether this project will ever see the light of day remains an open question, but I was delighted at the possibility to introduce my work and to receive such positive feedback. On reflection, I think that I made myself known to about a hundred people in all during my stay there. Such interaction would be simply inconceivable in Japan. Overall, it was an enriching period for me: I was able constantly to focus on my work while opening up future possibilities by meeting others working in the field.

Matsuda Naoki (April 2013)

Clothing / Crossing

Friday March 22nd to Sunday April 12th, 2013.
Treasure Hill Artist Village Attic Gallery

台湾には様々な博物館があります。その中で見た、原住民の衣装のひとつに、自分の過去の作品と似ているものがありました。それは、白い貝のようなものが全体に装飾されたものでした。それをきっかけに台湾の衣装について調べました。国立図書館での、1900年前後の原住民を記録した写真資料は圧巻でした。ある博物館では、原住民の風習や装飾品を造る工程などの映像を見ました。ビデオの前で子供たちはピースをしていて、おじいちゃんは頭を下げています。それは、普通の田舎の風景にも見え、とても親近感が湧きました。また、偶然にも私が興味を持った衣装の特集をやっている博物館があったので、実物を見に行きました。改めて、これを作った方の感性と、自分の制作での感性がシンクロしていることを強く感じました。他にも、台中で漢民族の文化を見たり、新しい文化施設で戦時中の映像資料を見たり、日本統治時代の文物館に行ったり、現代の街にある服屋を散策したり、出来るだけ幅広く台湾のことを知ろうと試みました。なぜなら、台湾を代表する衣装が特定できないことに気づいたからです。10種類以上いる原住民の衣装はバラバラで、漢民族以降のものは時代によって違います。そして、現在の台湾は日本にとても似ています。衣装のことを学ぶと、同時にその国の歴史を学ぶことが出来ます。台湾の歴史の時間と、私がスタジオでお米を並べて行った個人的な時間が作品上で交差するようなイメージでつくりました。

松田直樹(2013年3月)

During my stay in the Taiwanese capital I visited one of the city's many museums, which featured textile exhibits of indigenous origin - white shell-like pieces used decoratively - that resembled some of my previous work. This spurred me on to do further research on native Taiwanese costumes. Of particular interest were photographs of traditional costumes worn around the turn of the 20th century in the archives in the library of the National Museum. In another museum I had occasion to watch audio-visual files about the process involved in making traditional costumes and various local customs. One could see young children making peace signs while elderly craftsmen buried their heads in work. These images of pastoral landscapes struck me in such a way that I felt a very close sense of affinity with them. As it happened, another museum was exhibiting costumes in which I was deeply interested so I dropped along to see the real thing. I was once again deeply struck at the similarities in approach. I also took the opportunity to study and look at other Taiwanese cultural exhibits - not alone contemporary pieces and facilities but also archive footage of the war. Among locations I visited was the museum for relics from the time of the Japanese occupation. I walked Taipei's streets browsing the clothes shops, as I wanted to absorb as much local culture as possible. It struck me that it wasn't possible to pin down what was a representative Taiwanese clothing. There were at least ten different sorts of traditional costume, and depending on the era those produced after the Chinese style varied somewhat. In many ways contemporary Taiwan resembles Japan. In studying their approach to clothing, I was also able to gain better insight into that nation's history. I'm left with the impression that my work created during my residency there reflects the crossing point between a point of time in Taiwanese history and my personal time in the atelier spent laying out rice.

Matsuda Naoki (March 2013)

2012
台北 ⇒ 横浜
Taipe → Yokohama

Lo Yi-Chun
羅 懿君

1985年台北に生まれる。2007年国立台湾芸術大学彫刻科MFA取得。以後台湾各地で展覧会を行う。近年、日本、インド、オランダ、米国等で滞在制作を行い、サイトスペシフィックな作品を発表している。また、コミュニティや環境芸術プロジェクトに活動領域を広げている。2015年高雄賞を受賞。

Born in Taipei in 1985, Lo Yi-Chun received her MFA in Sculpture in 2007 from the National Taiwan University of the Arts. In recent years she has exhibited in Japan, India and the Netherlands and participated in a residency programme in the United States, where she created a site-specific works. She has expanded her artistic practice to community and environmental art projects. She was chosen for the 2015 Kaohsiung Award.

横浜での滞在について

わたしにとって、今回が初めての来日でした。だから最初、私は異なる環境の中できっとカルチャーショックを受けるのではないかと期待していました。しかし、横浜という都市の生活の中で出会う、街中の看板の漢字や道行く人たちの顔つき、コンビニのお菓子、Meiji、Pocky、Ghana等々、どれもわたしには見知ったものでした。わたしは、ことばを話さなければ、完全に人混みに紛れていることさえできました。

私は毎日自転車でラーメンを食べに行き、スーパーでにぎり寿司を買い、書店で雑誌を立ち読みし、銭湯にも行きました。しだいに私はこの見慣れた風景の中に、自分自身との繋がりを感じるようになり、自分の子どもの頃からの生活体験が蘇ってきました。日本と台湾は地理的に近く、歴史文化にも繋がりがあるので、日本文化は台湾人にとっては見知らぬものではなく、地続きの共通体験をしているかのようです。だから、私はこの表面的には見慣れた現象を今一度改めて注視しました。そして、バナナを媒介にして日本と台湾の歴史、経済、文化関係をリサーチすることにしたのです。

この作品創作のために地域の住民といろいろなコミュニケーションを持ったこと、またバンカートに滞在制作する間にたくさんの誠実な友人達に出会ったこと、折々の楽しいパーティに参加したり、帰国直前に満開の桜を見ることができたことなど、胸一杯の思い出を抱えて帰国しました。私は今こう思っています。この滞在制作が私にもたらしたのは、一時的なカルチャーショックなどではなく、心のなかで発酵を続ける内省と感動だったのだということを。

羅懿君(2012年4月)

Yokohama Residency

On my recent maiden trip to Japan, I somehow expected to suffer culture shock in a different environment to the one I am accustomed to in Taiwan. Reaching Yokohama, however, and seeing street and shop signs in Chinese charcters, familiar faces on the streets, familiar sweet brands such as Meiji, Pocky, Ghana and so forth in the convenience stores, it became clear that I could completely fit in and remain indistinguishable from the locals in the day-to-day bustle of this new environment - on condition, naturally, that I did not to speak.

My daily routine involved all sorts of typical Yokohama activities: riding a bicycle to a local ramen noodle restaurant, buying nigiri sushi at the supermarket, reading magazines at the book shop, and even going to the sentò, the local public bath. Over time I gradually began to feel within myself a connection to these cityscapes I was becoming accustomed to that somehow made me recall my childhood in Taiwan. Given the geographical proximity of Japan to Taiwan and close cultural ties, Japanese culture is not regarded as foreign, but rather as a shared experience between adjoining nations. This led me to one again carefully observe the ostensible aspect of such familiar phenomena. Availing of the banana plant and fruit as a vector, I decided to deepen my research into the cultural, historical and economical ties between Japan and Taiwan. So as to flesh out this body of work, I set about establishing contact with various groups in the local community. It is largely thanks to these encounters with true friends during my residency at BankART that I was able to participate in numerous social gatherings, and even enjoy the pleasure of seeing the cherry blossoms in full bloom just before returning to my homeland. As these warm memories still linger in my heart, it strikes me that the impact my residency had upon me was not of the order of a transient cultural shock but rather an incitement to continual self-examination and responsiveness.

Lo Yi-Chun (April 2012)

芭娜娜・バナナ・Saging
Banana in Taiwan, Japan and Philippines
March22 — April 14, 2012
BankART Studio NYK／Studio201

BankART Studio NYKでの滞在制作期間のうち、2月20日から3月20日まで、毎日定時に赤レンガ倉庫にあるレストランbillsに行き、バナナケーキを作った後に出るバナナの皮を回収しました。そしてそれを自然乾燥させ、平たく延ばし、昔の台中バナナ市場の写真を参考にしながら、1950年代の台湾バナナ市場の活況を表すインスタレーション作品を作りました。

バナナをリサーチ対象として選んだのは、バナナが日本で最も一般的な果物のひとつであり、輸入量が最も多い産品だからです。かつては、日本のバナナのほとんどは台湾から輸入されました。しかし1970年代になると、次第にフィリピン産バナナに取って代わられました。このポピュラーなフルーツは、私の台湾と日本での生活体験をつなぐものでありながら、今はあまり関心を持たれてないという印象を持ちました。この一見どれも似ているバナナは、異なった姿で私たちの眼前に拡げられ、また現在の流通システムの中で、それぞれの国の文化を語り、様々な思いを想起させるものです。この作品の素材は全てフィリピン産バナナですが、わたしはこれらによって昔日のバナナ王国、台湾の活況を思いおこし、さらにわたしが日本で見つけたバナナ商品をシニカルに配置しました。このプロジェクトによって、わたしは日常生活における消費(Consumption)と蓄積(Accumulation)をリサーチし、バナナという対象を借りて台湾と日本の歴史的なコンテクストの中で、現在も複雑に展開を続ける、市場における各国の関係を表そうとしました。

羅 懿君(2012年3月)

During my residency at Bankart Studio NYK, I created this work from banana peels which I collected from a nearby restaurant, Bills, every day between February 20th and March 20th. I dried and flattened these banana peels in order to weave a historical picture of the thriving banana market in Taiwan in the 1950s.

I am interested in the topic of bananas because it is one of the most popular and most imported fruits in Japan. In the early years, Japan had imported bananas from Taiwan, but after the 1970s, it has been replaced by the Philippines. Bananas link my daily experience from Taiwan to Japan, but they also bring up complicated feeling when I see numerous similar kinds of bananas everywhere in Japan. These bananas come from different nations and represent different cultures and images of nations under the market economy.

This work consists of many bananas peels from the Philippines, nevertheless, it represents the previously bustling banana market of Taiwan. In addition to discussing the historical market relationship between Taiwan, Japan and the Philippines, I was also exploring the consumption and accumulation in daily life through my participation.

Lo Yi-Chun (March 2012)

2013
横浜 ⇒ 台北
Yokohama → Taipei

Isozaki Michiyoshi
磯崎道佳

1968年水戸市生まれ。1996年多摩美術大学大学院修了。2001年 P.S.1/MoMAインターナショナルスタジオプログラムに参加。現在北海道在住。主なプロジェクトに、面識のない者同士による手紙の交換を目的とした「パラシュートとマキオ」(2002〜)。雑巾で等身大の動物を制作する「ぞうきんぞうプロジェクト」(2004〜)。参加者と巨大バルーンを協働制作する「ドーム/DOMEプロジェクト」(2005〜)。「笑う机」(2012〜)など。

Born in1968 in Mito, Isozaki completed his studies at the Tama Arts University postgraduate course in 1996. He participated in the 2001 PS1 / MoMA International studio program. *Parachute and Makio* (2002) aimed at an exchange of letters among people who are not acquainted with each other. *The Zokinzou Project* (2004) involved him creating life-sized animals from floor mops. Other prominent projects were *Dome Project* (2005) and *Laughing Desk* (2012).

TAVでの滞在について

台北国際松山空港から地下鉄で5駅、改札を出て徒歩数分で台北國際藝術村に到着した。まずその立地に驚いた。空港から30分以内、スタジオの窓からは台北駅とバスターミナルビルが見える。旧官庁街に元行政の建物をリノベーションしたレジデンス施設だ。台湾政府の行政院は1ブロック先、国会にあたる立法院は3ブロック先である。この立地のおかげで、これから歴史的な出来事を、台湾のアーティストや美術関係者のリアルな感情や動向と一緒に体験することになる。

滞在中のメインイベントになるオープンスタジオは3月22日(土)、23日(日)に行なわれた。同時期に「太陽花學運」(ひまわり学生運動)と呼ばれる学生運動が数ブロック先で始まった。3月18日(火)、台湾と中国による「両岸(台湾、中国)サービス貿易協定」の不透明な審議プロセスに抗議する形で、学生が立法院に不法侵入し占拠することになる。すぐにその動きに同調する形で、台湾のアーティストと美術関係者も運動を支持。3ブロック先の立法院前の座り込みに参加するようになる。友人も座り込みの途中ここにトイレを借りに度々立ち寄り、私のスタジオで休憩し、晩ご飯を一緒に食べに行くようになる。そして私も彼らの案内で座り込みの現場を訪れ、毎朝の散歩に現場へカメラを持って見て回るようになった。

そしてオープンスタジオの最終日の23日、行政院への不法侵入と占拠に対し、政府が強制排除を開始。その夜、台北國際藝術村の前では警察や救急車が常に動き回り、怪我をして避難して来た学生や、トイレを借りにやって警察、両者が入り乱れ、混沌とした状況になっていた。

そして、翌日から台北國際藝術村は政府によるバリケード区域内になり、アーティストも通行チェックが行なわれるようになった。しかし抗議行動はさらに学生主体から一般市民へ拡大し、3月30日には大規模なデモ行動(主催者側発表で約50万人)が行なわれた。美術関係者も現場にテントを建て、その広報やイメージ戦略にFacebookなどインターネットを活用し参加するようになる。そして当日のドキュメントをPVにし、続々インターネットで発表した。

私は抗議活動の終息を見ることなく、その約1週間後に帰国した。帰国前日、今回抗議活動に積極的に関わっている美術関係者の女性に尋ねたことがある。ここまで一般的に支持されている抗議活動に、何故ここまで関わるのか。彼女は、「台湾自体が少数派だから」と答えた。

私は、アートは多様性を示すのに適した表現だと思っている。そのため少数派とは相性が良い。体制側や多数派とアートが密接に関わると、あまり良い結果を生まないと思っていた。今回の滞在でまた大きな宿題をもらった気がしている。

磯崎道佳 (2014年4月)

About my residency at Taipei Artist Village

A mere five stops on the metro from the airport, and a few minutes walk from the nearest station, the Taipei Artist's Village's location really took me aback. Aside from the fact that is merely 30 minutes to the airport, one can see the Taipei railway station and central bus terminal from the studio window. The residency facilities are located in the former administrative district in a renovated government building. In terms of orientation, the Taiwanese government administrative building is just a block away, while the Legislative Yuan is another three blocks further on.

Thanks to its central location, one can experience history at first hand and get a real sense of the feelings and tendencies among Taiwanese artists and those involved in the art-world. During my residency an Open Studio was held on the weekend of March 22 and March 23. Coincidentally, on Tuesday March 18 the Sunflower Student Movement burst onto the scene several blocks away to protest against Cross-Strait Service Trade Agreement (CSSTA) between Taiwan and Mainland China in less than transparent circumstances. The students illegally occupied the Legislative Yuan. As a mark of solidarity, local artists and activists soon supported their actions and participated in the sit-in. Friends of mine who joined the students came sometimes to my studio to use the toilet, or to take a break and we would go out together in the evening to have dinner somewhere. Following their advise I visited the site of the sit-in, camera in hand and made it part of my morning walk.

On March 23, the final day of the Open Studio, the government deployed the police to forcibly expel the students from the occupied buildings. That evening, police and ambulance personnel were a constant presence in front of the Taipei Artist's Village; chaotic scenes resulted in the confusion between the injured students who had sought refuge and the police who entered to make use the building's toilet facilities. On the following day the Artist's Village was designated a barricaded zone by the government and artists entering the area were also subject to control.

In the meanwhile, however, the student protests gathered momentum and they gained the support of the city's residents leading to a massive demonstration on March 30, which according to the organisers attracted some 500,000 people. The artistic community also participated in the demonstration, erecting tents on the site, and also strategically availed of Facebook and the Internet to disseminate images of the demonstration. Since then, there was a constant live stream of the events day by day.

I was unable to witness the final days of the protest movement because I returned to Japan about a week after the demonstration. Before departing Taiwan, I was able to visit a lady in the art world who was actively involved in the protest movement. I asked her why you were involved actively in the protests that is so generally supported. She replied: "In Taiwan itself, a minority." I am of the opinion that art is a suitable vehicle for expressing diversity, and, as such, is compatible with a minority perspective. I thought that when art is directly related to the majority and establishment, the results are less than satisfactory. I can't help feeling that my recent residency in Taipei leaves me with many unanswered questions to ponder over.

Isozaki Michiyoshi (April 2014)

「笑う鏡 smile in the mirror」

ほとんどの人が、毎朝、鏡に映る自分の顔と儀式のように対面している。女性は化粧をし、男性はヒゲを剃る。鏡に映るその姿は他者と共有することはない。家族や愛する人にでさえ見せることがない無防備な自分だけの姿/顔の確認作業。朝の鏡には誰に向けるでもない個人的な微笑みが刻印されていると感じている。震災と原発事故以降、「笑顔」の社会における機能について考えている。特に子どもたちにとって笑うことは大切だが、彼らの笑顔を一番必要としているのは誰なのか。笑うことが難しくなったと感じる現代、改めて笑顔の役割、機能について考えている。今回、このプロジェクトには3カ所で撮影した人々の笑顔をモチーフにしている。茨城県守谷市にあるホットスポットとして放射線量が高くなってしまった小学校の子どもたち。私の地元の北海道の学生。そして台湾の子どもたちの笑顔である。私のレジデンスの担当者にお願いし、人が多く集まる商業施設に連れて行ってもらい、一般の方に笑顔の撮影の協力をお願いした。次に約100個の手鏡を台北で購入し、鏡の裏側の銀メッキを引っ掻いて剥がし、笑顔のドローイングを刻印した。

「パラシュートとマキオ：宇和島-台北-横浜」

私が継続し行なっている参加型プロジェクトである。参加者に手のひらサイズの手作りパラシュートを作ってもらい、面識のない人に向けた手紙をつけてもらう。その「お手紙付きパラシュート」を集め、私がメッセンジャーになり次の場所でパラシュートを放ち、参加者に拾ってもらう。

今回の台北滞在に前後して、愛媛県宇和島市を訪ねることが決まっていたので、まず宇和島市で台北の人に向けた「お手紙付きパラシュート」を集め、オープンスタジオの会場で来て頂いた台湾の人に、宇和島市からの「お手紙付きパラシュート」を渡した。次に彼らに面識のない日本人に向けた、「お手紙付きパラシュート」を作ってもらった。

磯崎道佳（2014年4月）

Smile in the Mirror

Almost everybody in ritual fashion comes to face with his or her own face in the mirror each morning. Women do their make-up while men shave themselves. The image reflected in the mirror is not one that is shared with others. Even family members or lovers don't get a chance to get a glimpse of this daily confirmation of one's unguarded face/image. It is as though this engraved personal smile in the morning mirror is not directed at anyone. Ever since the earthquake and subsequent nuclear accident in March 2011, I have been constantly thinking of the social function of the "smile". For children laughing is especially important but one has to ask who is most in need of their smile? In an age when it feels increasingly difficult to laugh, I am once again examining the societal function and role of the smile.

For this project I photographed people smiling in three separate locations. The first was a group of elementary school pupils in Moriya in Ibaraki prefecture, a spot where radiation levels had become alarmingly high. The next group was a group of students from my native Hokkaido. And, finally the smiles of children in Taiwan. I asked the staff member of TAV if it would be possible to take me to a commercial centre where many people gather and to ask passers-by if they would smile for the camera. My next step was to purchase about a hundred hand mirrors in Taipei, and to remove the silver-plating at the back of the mirror and to imprint a drawing of a smile in its place.

Parachute and Makio:
Uwajima -Taipei - Yokohama.

This on-going participatory project in which I ask the participants to make a homemade palm-sized parachute and subsequently have them attach a letter to someone they have never met to it. I collect the parachutes with the attached letters, and somewhat like a messenger release the parachutes at the next location I visit where I have them picked up by participants. About the time of my Taipei residency it had been decided that I would visit Uwajima in Ehime prefecture. I first of all collected the parachutes with the attached letters from the residents of Uwajima for the residents of Taipei. During my Open Studio days at the Artist's Studio, I distributed them to the visitors. I then had them make parachutes to which they could attach their letters to Japanese people they had never met.

Isozaki Michiyoshi (April 2014)

2013
台北 ⇒ 横浜
Taipe → Yokohama

Yang Tzu-Hung
楊 子弘

1985年台南に生まれる。国立交通大学応用芸術研究所修士。彫刻、インスタレーション、コンセプチュアルアートを手がける。ふだんは見過ごされているが、人々の知覚に深く関与する日常生活の物事に焦点をあて、作品化することで新たな様相を眼前に描き出す。2014年BankART滞在制作中に起きたサンフラワー運動以来、台湾の政治状況に関わる作品制作を始めた。

Born in Tainan in 1985, Yang Tzu-Hang earned his Masters Degree from National Chiao Tung University of Applied Arts. His work principally revolves around sculpture, installation and conceptual art, dealing with that which we overlook in our everyday lives but that hinders our perception. Since his residency in 2014 at BankART, he has begun creating works that touch upon Taiwan's political reality.

横浜に滞在して

このたびのレジデンスは、わたしの人生最初の滞在制作だった。子どもの頃沖縄に行ったことがあるが、その印象は今はほとんど覚えてない。だから、記憶している範囲では、はじめて日本に来たようなものだった。自分にとって、日本の感覚はいつも新鮮であり、同時に熟知したもののようでもある。台湾では、つねに日本の様々の文化に接していた。たとえば、日本食、マンガ、テレビ番組など。横浜で接するものには、私にとって、頭のどこかに既視感があり、日本に対して何とも言えない特別な感情がある。

滞在していた場所であるBankART Studio NYKは、横浜港の近くに位置し、東京のような人混みとは様子が違う。わたしは、こんなすこしがらんとした雰囲気が好きだ。ここで生活すると、日本で最初に開港した港・横浜の西洋的な雰囲気を感じることができる。道を歩くと、沢山の西洋建築と賑やかな中華街が融合している。ここはずっと昔から文化のるつぼだったのだと言うことが理解できる。たいへん幸運なことに、BankART1929が新・港区のスタジオを撤収する前に、その巨大な空間を訪れ、多くのアーティスト達と交流する機会を得た。ともに芸術を語り、日本の芸術家の創作についていっそう深く理解することができた。このようなことは、最も直接的で、実際的な文化交流だった。

また、この滞在期間中に、参禅や寺社詣でもした。そして、日本の神道の深い精神性についても幾ばくかの理解を得ることができた。ちょうど滞在中に台湾では「サンフラワー学生運動」が起きた。そのことがあり、わたしは成果発表の際、この運動を出発点に作品を創作した。そして、日本の宗教でよく行われる、手に蝋燭を持って洞窟に入る習慣を取り入れ、観覧者に蝋燭を持って展示を見てもらい、台湾の未来を共に祈った。

楊 子弘（2014年4月）

Yokohama Residency

This was my first experience of a residency programme. As a child I had been to Okinawa, but I hardly remember anything of the time I was there. So, in that sense my trip to Yokohama was like my maiden trip to Japan. My impressions of Japan are fresh, and yet they are also familiar to me in another way. I was already acquainted with Japan and Japanese culture in Taipei: I eat Japanese cuisine, read Manga and watch Japanese TV channels. On reaching Yokohama, I had a sense of déjà vu and somehow felt as though there was an indescribable link between Japan and I. My residency at the BankART Studio NYK was located close to the Yokohama waterfront. Unlike Tokyo, Yokohama is nowhere nearly as congested and I really enjoy this somewhat open atmosphere in the city. My residency there enabled me to get a sense of Yokohama's maritime legacy, with its port and its western feel. Taking a stroll about the city, one sees a lot of western architecture and fashion and yet within a few steps further one finds oneself in bustling Chinatown. It is as though it has been a cultural melting pot down throughout the years.

As good fortune would have it, before BankART1929 left its studio in Shin Minato-ku, I had the opportunity to visit that tremendous space, and to come into contact and exchange opinions with numerous local artists. In discussing art with them, I was able to come to a deeper understanding of Japanese artists and their work. Thanks to these frank discussions, genuine culture exchanges could take place. Moreover, during my sojourn in Yokohama, I had occasion to visit temples and participate in Zen meditation. I was able to grasp the deeply religious nature of Shinto. During my stay in Yokohama, the Sunflower Student Movement was happening in Taiwan. Given these circumstances, the pieces I created for my exhibition at the close of my Yokohama residency took their cue from this movement. As is common practice in Japanese religious rituals whereby a lighted candle is placed in the hand before entering a cave, I had the spectators at the exhibition hold up a candle to my work, and prayed together with them for Taiwan's future.

Yang Tzu-Hung (April 2014)

立会人 / 見證者 / The Witness

April 18 - 20, 2014.
BankART Studio NYK, Studio 201

遠方にあっても、あたかも現場に身を置いているように、「見證者」(立会人)となる。事件の発生というのは、しばしば過去の事象が累積し、ジグソーパズルが次第次第にできあがっていくかのように起きるものだ。遠い故国の民主主義が挑戦と威嚇を受ける状況にあって、318サンフラワー学生運動が、台湾の、今や闇に飲み込まれようとしている民主主義に灯火をともした。自分は異国にあって、直接参加することはできない。それでも、心は故郷につながっている。この体はその場から引き離されているが、遠い現場にある、真実で血が滴る存在を眺めるとき、はたして「真実」とは何なのか、考えさせられる。メディア情報が限られた日本で、多くの人々は、ネットを通して、また親しい友人達のコメントを通して状況の一端を理解する。メディアを通じていては、今台湾で現に起きていることを知ることはできない。しかし、芸術の実践を通すとき、「サンフラワー学生運動」はもはや画面上の他人事ではなく、現在進行中の出来事になる。今回の展示は、見る人を一同に立会人として、この遠いところで起きていることに近しく関与し、思索するためのものである。日本の寺院には洞窟をもつものがあり、僧侶や信徒の修行の場となっている。洞窟のもつ闇は、恐れと不安を感じさせる。手に蝋燭をもち、小さな灯火が眼になると同時に、心を平穏に保つ支えになる。昔と変わらず、電灯を使わずに、蝋燭を唯一の光りの手引きとすることは、蝋燭の宗教に対する重要な位置づけを表している。手に蝋燭を持てば、早足で歩くことはできず、風で消えることも避けながら、静かに歩行する。重大な変化はさっさと成し遂げられるのではなく、時間の中で人間の身体行動を通じてゆっくりと変わっていくことを示唆しているかのようだ。光りを持って洞窟に入る。前方を照らす。自分を照らす。他人を照らす。光りは、眼を代用するだけではなく、心を寄せる物事に対する祈りであり、敬いであり、希望と平和をもたらす。サンフラワーは、永遠に光りに向かい、闇の中の光りを求め、前進を続ける。遠方の立会人は、事件の現場を間近に見ることができない。しかし、頭で事実を理解するだけでなく、心に導かれ、自分の現在との関わりを思考し、非暴力のエネルギーを祈り、過去と、現在と未来に立ち会う。

楊 子弘 (2014年4月)

Even at a distance one can become an observer or a witness just like somebody who is close at hand to the incident. Events often happen as though the result of the cumulative effect of various phenomena, like the assorted pieces of a jigsaw puzzle being assembled. In the current situation in which the democratic bedrock of my distant homeland is subject to intimidation and aggression, the 318 Sunflower Student Movement are a beacon of hope for Taiwanese democracy that is currently being enveloped in darkness. Given that I am at present overseas, I am unable to participate directly. Yet my heart is deeply connected to my homeland and what is happening there. Any while physically separated, the fact of looking at the situation from afar – and all the more so when I actually see blood being shed – makes me question what is the truth of the matter. In Japan, information concerning events on the ground is scarce, and most people inform themselves through the Internet or by reading blogs and commentaries by close friends. It is not actually possible to grasp what is currently happening in Taiwan through media outlets. However, in the artistic practice the Sun Flower Student Movement, the image we witness is no longer an event that is only of concern to others, but rather one that is happening right now and with direct impact on our lives. My current exhibition involves each and every spectator being and becoming an observer, reflecting and becoming engaged with events that are taking place far away. There is a Japanese temple in which the monks and laity alike use a cave as a training ground. This cave's darkness engenders both fear and anxiety. While holding a candle in one's hand, the mind becomes calm as the faint lamplight strikes the eye. Nothing has changed since the old days; they still do not use electric light, and the fact of being guided by candlelight represents the deeply religious significance of the candle. When holding a lit candle, it is impossible to hurry along; one has to protect it from the wind and one is constrained to walk slowly. What is hereby suggested is that significant changes are not achieved at breathing-taking pace but rather physical behaviour changes gradually over time. We enter the cave bearing light. We shine a light on what lays ahead. We also illuminate ourselves in the process, and those around us. Light is a quality that not only substitutes the eye, but also is a source of peace, prayer, honour and grace. The sunflower continues to press forward, shedding light upon the darkness, casting light into eternity. And while a distant observer is unable to witness what is actually happening on the ground, he or she nonetheless can be guided by their hearts – and not necessarily only intellectually understand the situation – and thus reflect upon their own current situation, and pray for a resolution through non-violent energy, while observing the past, present and future.

Yang Tzu-Hung (April 2014)

2014
横浜 ⇒ 台北
Yokohama → Taipei

SUNDRUM
サンドラム

2010年結成。2011年「BankARTLife 3-新港村」に出演。2012年「越後妻有大地の芸術祭閉会式」に出演。2014年「BankARTLife4-東アジアの夢」パレードでの演奏、2週間の滞在制作、単独公演。2015年、BankARTの横浜台北交流事業で台湾に滞在。THAVアートランタンフェスティバルで公演。

Formed in 2010, Sundrum participated in the 2011 in the BankART Life 3 - Shin Minatomura. In 2012, they performed at the closing ceremony at the Echigo-Tsumari Art Triennale. In 2014, they played in the street parade during BankART Life 4 - East Asian Dream. As part of the BankART Yokohama Taipei exchange programme they had a residency in Taipei. They performed at the THAV Art Lantern Festival.

Sundreaming Life in Taiwan

音楽という言葉は、音楽が音楽単体で切り離されたときにできたのだろう。うたやおどりはそれよりずっと前からある。台湾原住民は太古の昔からその姿を今に伝えている。

原住民の部落に滞在すると、よく皆酒を呑んで歌っている。これは先祖からずっとそうやって歌い踊り継がれてきた事なので、原住民の酒、小米酒(シャオミーチョウ)などを一緒に呑んで歌い続けていると、その一族と同じ世界に入っていく。そうすると、時間をこえて、夢と現実の境もこえている。先祖の知恵を共有し、遥かな時間へ、神話の世界まで現実と繋がっている。

この旅は、「Sundreaming Life in Taiwan」と名付けた。メンバーが少しずつ集まり、台湾原住民と共に過ごし歌う事で、パフォーマンス、ステージ、うた、音楽、踊りとは何かを一から考え直し、その原点の感覚で、SUNDRUMが旅をし、公演をし、生活するという作品だ。

SUNDRUM(2015年7月)

Sundreaming Life in Taiwan

As for the term "music", mankind has succeeded in uncoupling it from the simple substance of music. Long before it ever did so with song and dance. The Taiwanese aborigines continue incorporating that ancient tradition.

If you visit an aboriginal hamlet, you will observe how to this day everyone still sings and drinks alcohol. The tradition of dancing and singing has been handed down from their forefathers, so by continuing to drink the local liquor – Xiaomijiu – and sing together, they collectively embark into the same world. There, beyond time, they also transcend the frontiers between dream and reality. Sharing the wisdom of their ancestors, they connect to a far-off time, linking their everyday reality to the world of mythology.

We called this journey "Sundreaming Life in Taiwan". Members gradually assemble, and the fact we spend time together singing with the Taiwanese aborigines, offers an occasion to fundamentally rethink the meaning of our performances, stage-work, songs, music and dance. With these origins in mind, SUNDRUM embarks on a journey, to perform publically and to create an artwork called life.

SUNDRUM (July 2015)

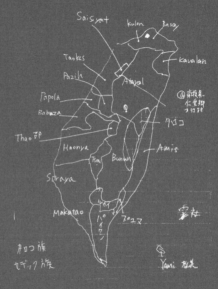

BankART Life Theater
SUNDRUM SUNDREAMING LIFE in BankART
2015年8月25日[月]、31日[日]
BankART Studio NYK
仮面制作：井坂奈津子

2014
台北 ⇒ 横浜
Taipe → Yokohama

Hsu Chiao-Yen
許 喬彦

1990年嘉義市に生まれる。朝陽科技大学インテリアデザイン科卒業、国立台南芸術大学造形研究所在籍。人間の記憶した「出来事の痕跡」が時間とともにどのように変化するかをミクストメディアによるインスタレーションで表現。また、インパクトのある言葉を駆使しながら、人間の古い記憶の中にある「原型」を再構成する作品を制作している。

Born in Chia-yi city in 1990, Hsu Chiao-Yen enrolled at the Tainan National University of the Arts after graduating from the Chaoyang University of Technology Interior Design faculty. His mixed-media installations examine the transformations of memory and how it "traces events". Exploiting words with impact, he creates artworks to reconstruct our "prototype" memories.

縛られて、漂う

今回の横浜滞在は、自分自身の人生ではじめて海外でレジデンスする経験だった。また、一人旅も初めてのことだった。わたしは、期待に胸を膨らませ、日本の、横浜のBankART1929に到着した。近くの日本式アパートに落ち着き、日本人の日常生活を体験することがスタートした。

わたしは毎日住まいとバンカートとの間を歩いて行き来しながら、小さな店の入り口に、のぼり旗が立てられ、宣伝や看板になっているのを目にした。そんな店の一つに入って買い物すると、出るときにはいつもプラスチックバッグを手にしている。パンひとつ、ミネラルウォーター1本だというのに。そこで、毎日の生活で手にするプラスチックバッグを集めてみることが、わたしの楽しみになった。そこに、この場所の文化の細部を嗅ぎ取ることができた。

私はあるとき近くの神社を訪れた。すると、そこにも無数の幟旗が風にはためいて、そこら中に立てられているではないか。旗には、献金をした人ひとりびとりの名前が記されている。この光景は、精神性のある儀式のようでもあり、またリアルな情報伝達が効率よく成される様のようでもある。思うに、幟は何より日常の情報伝達と告知機能を持っている。形象と文字が一体となって、たえず揺れながら近づき遠のく、情報の運び手である。しかしそこには、物質的消費だけでなく、崇高な精神性のある隠喩も潜んでいる。見方を変えれば、幟は、短く、また長い記憶をとどめているのだと思う。そこで、私は幟を創作の素材にすることにした。環境と融合したインスタレーション作品として、私が今回の滞在制作で得た、精神と生活における経験の一コマとしたい。

許 喬彦(2015年4月)

GO or STAY

It is the first experience in my life that I joined in the overseas artist residency program. Moreover, in fact it's the first time for me to travel abroad alone. With a full of hope and happy expectation for the unknown land and people, I arrived at Yokohama's BankART1929 and settled down in the Japanese house with tatami in its neighborhood. Thus, my new daily life in Japan started eventually.

While I go back and forth on foot in the area between BankART and my flat everyday, I found the *Nobori* (banner flag) for the advertisement at many of small stores entrance in the street. Whenever I shop something in such a store, the salespersons pack the things neatly in the plastic bag, even for a piece of bread or a bottle of mineral water. It became my joyful custom to collect the plastic bags that I was given in the daily shopping. I actually was interested in the cultural details in situ that I felt in such trivial matters.

One day I dropped by a Shinto shrine nearby. Then I found a lot of nobori installed in the precincts, waving in the wind everywhere. On each flag, the names of those who donated were written down. It looked like the religious ceremony and at the same time functioned as the practical and effective advertisement of information. The noboris, before all, are the media to transfer the code and tell what it includes. They always stand still and convey the integrated design of form and content, wherever we see them. However that's no all. They connote the highly spiritual metaphors as well as diffuse the commercial advertisement. In a sense, the noboris are the media for containing the human memories even though they are seen only temporarily.

I decided to use the noboris for my artwork during the residency. The installation can be outdoors and environmental but will mark the fresh experience that I had in the everyday and spiritual life in Japan.

Hsu Chiao-Yen (April 2015)

2008 Special Recognition
横浜 ⇒ 台北
Yokohama → Taipei
關渡美術館
Kuandu Museum of Fine ART

Maruyama Junko
丸山純子

1976年山梨県生まれ。ニューヨーク市立大学ハンターカレッジ美術学科卒。2004年「食と現代美術」(BankART Stuido NYK)。2005年「北仲OPEN!」事務局代表、以降横浜で活動。2006年「越後妻有大地の芸術祭」。2007年 Landmark Project II (NYK)。2007年 公益信託大木記念美術家助成基金受賞。2008年 Field of Ideas（オーストラリア）。2014年個展「漂泊界」(下山の森発電所美術館)。

Born in Yamanashi prefecture in 1986, she graduated from the Hunter College New York. In 2004, she participated in "Food and Contemporary Art" at BankART Studio NYK. In 2005, she became a representative of the office staff at "Kitanaka OPEN!". In 2006, she participated at the Echigo Tsumari Art Triennale. The Ohki Memorial Charitable Trust Fund awarded her a grant for artists in 2007. The following year (2008) she presented Field of Ideas in Australia. In 2014 she gave a solo exhibition Hyohakukai at the Power Plant Museum of Nizayama.

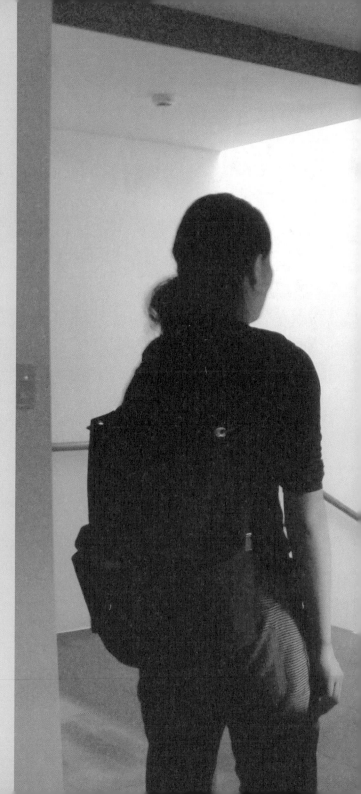

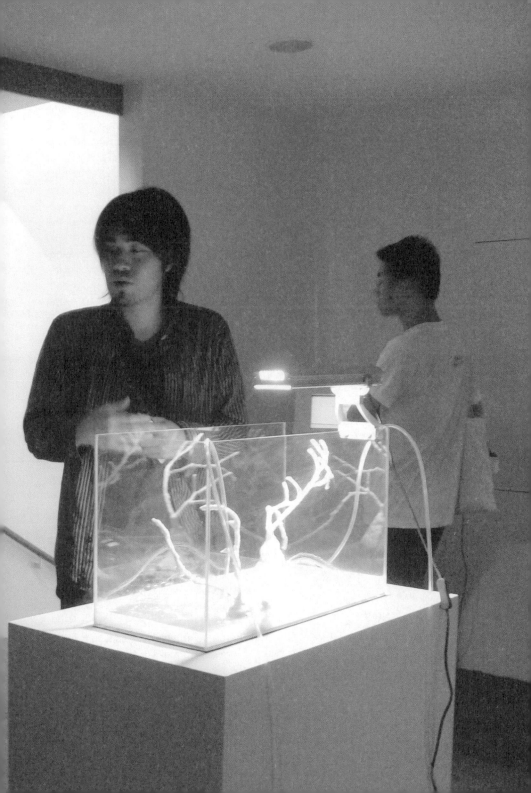

台北での滞在について

私は、BankARTにアーティストインレジデンスしていたホーさんと桜荘で出会いました。そのご縁でホーさんの働くKuandu Museum of Fine ARTに招待して頂きました。

Kuandu Museum of Fine ARTは、大学の敷地内にある美術館です。敷地内には食堂、売店、教師の宿舎等様々な施設が充実していました。

宿泊させて頂いたのは教師の宿舎で、清潔な広々とした空間でした。

また、制作場所として別の棟の広々とした屋上に繋がるスタジオを用意してくださいました。制作に必要な素材を揃えるのもも外国人には分かるはずも無い台湾の込み入ったショップで用意してくださいました。。そこで私は、食堂から油を貰い、石鹸を作り、沢山の実験的な作品を作らせてもらいました。また、花屋の花を学生さん達とともに作り、ショップで花を販売し、販売した売り上げで、みんなで猫が沢山いるカフェに行きました。

その後私は帰国しましたが、その後もおかせて頂いた花屋の花の売り上げで花を一緒に作ったメンバーはハンバーガーを食べに行ったと伝えてくれました。

メンバーで学校中を練り歩き花屋の宣伝をしたことを思い出します。

パオパオというアシスタントはその後美術普及の方向を目指していると伝えてくれました。

滞在時のスタッフは好意的で台湾料理屋さんや、観光スポットに連れて行ってくれました。バンカートから生まれたご縁で大変恵まれたアーティストインレジデンスの機会を頂き感謝しております。ありがとうございます。

丸山純子 (2009年7月)

About my residency at Taipei

The starting point that I was involved in the Taipei residency program was that I met Ho-san who was invited to the residency program from Taipei to Yokohama. I came across her at BankART Sakura-so. It is she that invited me to Kuandu Museum of Fine Art where she worked as curator.

The Kuandu Museum of Fine Art is built within the University. There are shops, restaurants and library in that area. I was staying in the large and clean dormitory for the teaching staff and they offered me a studio connected to the roof top of next building. The Kdmofa staff took me to the shop in the small street that no foreigner could find. During the stay, I got the used oil from the restaurant in campus and made it into soap, as well as had the opportunities to do lots of experimental things.

I also worked for the Flower Project with students and sold the flower at the shop. Then we went to the café having a lot of cats and spent there the income from the flower sales. After I came back to Japan, they told me that they even bought the hamburger with the income they made.

I remember that we walked with other members throughout the collage for advertising the Maruyama Florist. An assistant curator named Paopao said to me that she was studying the outreach program for the fine art in doing so.

The Kdmofa staff were very kind and took me to the Taiwanese restaurant and tourist spot. Thanks to the connection created by BankART program, I was given the opportunity for the artist in residency in Kdmofa and am very grateful for all that made it happen.

Maruyama Junko (July 2007)

2015.7.15/ BankART Studio NYK

台北市・横浜市の都市間交流事業について

横浜市は、「創造都市（クリエイティブ・シティ）」の実現を目指し、文化芸術の創造性を活かして都市の新しい価値や魅力につなげていく取り組みを進めており、都心臨海部を中心に、アーティストやクリエーターが創作・発表・滞在（居住）しやすい環境づくりを推進しています。また、横浜市は、世界に開かれた国際都市として、アジア諸都市等とのネットワークづくりに取り組んでおり、パートナー都市である台北市とは、芸術文化、スポーツ、図書館などさまざまな分野での交流を進めています。芸術分野では、平成17年度から、芸術家支援の分野などで国際的に豊富な実績をもつ台北市との間で、芸術家を相互に派遣する「芸術家交流事業」をスタートし、それぞれの都市から派遣された芸術家が、市民や現地の芸術関係者との交流を深めています。

横浜市文化観光局

TAIPEI and YOKOHAMA Artist Exchange Programme

A key objective of the Yokohama Creative City project has been to consolidate efforts from all sectors of the community to create an urban environment imbued with both charm and merit for resident and visitor alike. Combincultural legacy with its innate creativity, principally in the harbour and coastal areas, ing the city's artistic and the city authorities have continually nurtured an environment in which artists and the creative community can readily implement their projects, give vent to their expressive talents and set up residence. Moreover, given its geographical position and historical significance, Yokohama has continually remained open to the world, committed to strengthening existing ties and expanding networks with other Asian metropolis. Taipei, as a partner city in this enterprise, has likewise been actively engaged with Yokohama, and steadily encouraged various cultural and artistic projects, including sports and contact between libraries. In 2005, an artist's exchange programme was initiated, which over the years has ultimately led to more frequent and a deepening of the relationship between the citizens and all sectors of the artistic communities in both cities.

Yokohama Culture and Tourism Bureau

アートと都市を巡る

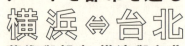

藝術與都市 橫濱與台北
Art and City in Yokohama and Taipei

2015 年 7 月 24 日 第一刷発行

編集	BankART1929
デザイン	北風総貴
翻訳	ジョン・バレット、張穎
印刷製本	株式会社シナノ
発行	BankART1929
	〒231-0002 横浜市中区海岸通 3-9
	TEL 045-663-2812 FAX 045-663-2813
	info@bankart1929.com

First edition on the 24th of July, 2015

Edited	BankART1929
Designed	Nobutaka Kitakaze
Translated	John Barrett, Zhang Ying
Printed	SHINANO Co, Ltd in Japan
Published	BankART1929
	3-9 Kaigandori, Naka-ku,
	Yokohama, Kanagawa 231-0002
	info@bankart1929.com

© BankART1929 All rights reserved

乱丁・落丁はお取り替えいたします。 ISBN978-4-902736-38-0 C3070 ¥1,000E